MW00334643

OWNING LAND MADE EASY

Jet Abuda-Sison

Jet Abuda-Sison/Owning Land Made Easy
Printed in the United States of America

Owning Land Made Easy/ Jet Abuda-Sison. -- 1st ed.

ISBN 978-0-692-82037-7 Print Edition

CONTENTS

Acknowledgments

I am forever grateful to all who selflessly taught, mentored, and shared with me their knowledge and life experiences. To my family, friends and all that I had the privilege to meet, THANK YOU! You all have made my journey much, much more interesting, colorful, and joyful.

INTRODUCTION

"Mr. Abuda, your house is burning!"

It was during an Easter celebration with my family and most of the town of Sipocot, Philippines when I heard those words. I was five years old, but the moment will forever remain seared in my memory.

My parents, brother, sister, and I ran across our small town to find our beloved home not just engulfed in flames, but a pile of smoking, charred wood. The only structure left standing was our burning staircase.

In shock, sobbing, and wearing what was soon to be our only clothing, we waited helplessly for the embers to cool so we could pick through the acrid ashes of our family home for anything we could still use. Owning fire insurance policies in our town was uncommon then, so all we had left was whatever we could find. The few coins we recovered were the remnants of the education fund my mom had been stowing away for years.

There was little else.

We weren't wealthy before the fire, but we had more than necessary. We even had enough money to afford doting maids. While you didn't have to be among the richest in the country for this luxury, we definitely lived more comfortably than most. After the fire that had spread from our next-door neighbor's, everything changed. In an instant, we literally had no material possessions left. Luckily, we still had the most important thing: each other.

We also had the land where our house once stood. After staying with our parents' friend for a few weeks, we returned back home, or I should say, back onto our land, as soon as my parents managed to put up four new posts, the skeleton of what would be our new house. From there, they began to buy materials: roofing panels, wood floors, etc., as quickly as their very limited budget would allow. The fire was a huge setback. We not only had to rebuild, we also had to buy everything all over again—furniture, cookware, clothes, and more. For what felt like the longest time, I dozed off to sleep in a makeshift bed, under a mosquito net, gazing at the stars above our unfinished roof.

Starting all over again was difficult and it put a great financial constraint on our family, but it made us stronger in our desires and convictions. Our parents, who both came from families of teachers, instilled in us the importance of education from a very young age. While others would probably consider rebuilding their home a priority, my mom and dad remained focused on giving us the best education possible. There were times when my parents had to borrow money from neighbors or mortgage the land to pay our tuition fees and other expenses. Their resolve never weakened. As a result, my siblings and I became more determined to finish our studies and support our parents who, despite having lost everything, never wavered in their resolve to send us to the best schools.

After seeing how losing everything affected my parents, I felt the need to do something to help them. Since I was still young, all I could do was imagine and dream about the many things I would do and accomplish for our family. When I was nine years old, I saw a picture of a Porsche in one of the *Reader's Digest* magazines my uncle brought home when he was on leave from the U.S. Navy. I promised my dad that someday, we would own a Porsche and drive him in it wherever he wanted to go. Since a carabao harnessed to a wagon was still a common mode of transportation at that time, my dream had to seem entirely farfetched.

Nevertheless, my dad and my grandfather, who were two of my favorite people, encouraged my wild dreams and went along for the imaginary ride. They always listened to my elaborate scenarios about the spoils we would one day afford. I promised my dad we would not only have a big new house, but multiple houses. He never made fun or discouraged me. Instead, he assured me that with determination and hard work, no goal was too lofty. To this day, I believe that telling my father and grandfather my childhood aspirations set my mind and body in motion toward whatever I needed to do.

Before the fire, my dad would harvest jackfruit, guava, young coconut, bananas, star apple, pineapple, sugar cane, and other tropical fruit that grew on our property, and share the surplus with our friends and neighbors. After the fire, we couldn't afford to be so generous, so we sold any extra fruit from a little stand we made in front of our forever work-in-progress home. We also helped my mom open a little storefront on one of the walls of our home, where we sold other household items.

It was my first delicious taste of entrepreneurship. I soon expanded my budding empire by buying boxes of candy and selling the pieces at school, which made me a few pesos profit per box. When I finally made enough capital, I would buy another box for a friend who would sell them for me, and I would give him or her half of the profit. Because of my little ventures, I seldom had to ask for an allowance. I was also able to give away some candies to classmates who couldn't afford to buy them. Having lost everything, I knew how it felt to have nothing, and I felt the need to share and help others whenever I could. Some of my fondest memories are of sharing and eating candies while I played with my childhood friends.

Early on, my mom took me along with her to teach in a near-by town. She was my first-grade teacher. We did not have the best schools in our small town, so once we finished elementary school, my parents sent us to nearby Naga City for secondary school. For my first year in high school, I enrolled at the University of Nueva Caceres (UNC).

Despite my entrepreneurial sensibilities, I initially wanted to pursue a career in journalism, but my dad thought it would've been a risky move since the country was under martial law. Instead, my father managed to convince me that it would be beneficial to have a doctor in the family. Upon graduation from high school, I was accepted at the University of Santo Tomas (UST) in Manila, one of the best medical schools in the country.

On the rare trips I could afford to go back home, I would buy as many pili nuts (a delicious and very rare nut that only grows in my hometown) as possible. When I returned to UST, I sold them to classmates who anticipated and loved eating this delicacy. With the extra profits earned from selling them, I had enough money for my everyday school expenses, and at times, enough left over to buy soap and toothpaste to give to prisoners at the jail where I sometimes volunteered.During summer break from college, I started working for some of the biggest rent-a-car companies in Manila. I enjoyed my position and the inherent challenge of making commission-based sales. Since I was limited by the length of my summer break, I tried to maximize my time by making as many sales as possible. I totally enjoyed and embraced the business world.

While I liked the idea of becoming a doctor to help people, I came to realize that I was studying diligently during the school year partly so I wouldn't let my family down, but mainly so I would have my summers free to work part time. Being in a sales environment and creating long-term business relationships satisfied my need to succeed in a way that being a doctor could not. Not for me, anyway.

Not long after college graduation, my husband, a machinist in the U.S. Navy, proposed and we got married. Together, we hopped on an airplane headed across the globe for a new journey in the United States of America.

We had our start in New London, Connecticut, where he was employed as a machinist at one of the naval shipyards. I was looking for work and, despite great recommendations from companies I'd worked for, getting that first job in the States proved to be challenging. The only place willing to hire me without any local references was a gas station. Just so I could get my first local job experience, I accepted a position as cashier. Like many immigrants, I started out with an arduous commute that included a forty-five-minute drive through a very unfamiliar weather condition—snow.

Two weeks later, a managerial position opened up in a clothing store in New London. Few weeks after that, I was hired at Budget Rent-a-Car and had my first office job in the States.

I have to admit, there was more than one moment when I contemplated going home to the Philippines to take up my abandoned career in medicine. However, my husband received a transfer order, and instead of calling it quits, we decided to seek our fortunes in San Diego, California.

While California's climate was better than I could've ever dreamt of, my dreams for success were still far from coming true. Starting over in a new city and soon to have our first child, I wanted to be able to help provide for our growing family. While working part time for the local school district, I enrolled in classes to learn office procedures. Upon completion, I took and passed civil service examinations and began to submit applications. I quickly received calls for interviews, received job offers, and chose a job at the San Diego Assessor's office.

I started by doing clerical work, but continued to take more civil service exams to qualify for higher positions. As I worked my way up the ladder, I learned how appraisals were done, understood the meaning of assessed values, supplemental taxes, and how to read parcel maps. While working at the Assessor's office, I had the opportunity to meet and talk to some of the county's big taxpayers. I realized that they weren't much different from the rest of us. One thing I noticed they had in common was that most had invested in, and developed, land. I also saw how land and real estate were just as valuable here in America as they were in the Philippines.

I thought about how significant a role my father's small piece of land played in sending my siblings and me to school, and how my parents were not able to afford any more properties. These thoughts may have created a subconscious decision that owning land in America, the richest country in the world, would be impossible. If our family could not afford to buy any more land in the Philippines beyond what we already had, then how could I, an immigrant, possibly afford to own here, especially in Southern California?

To supplement our growing family's income, and to satisfy my entrepreneurial bent, I started selling designer clothes to friends from the trunk of my car, and at home on weekends. I also started doing word processing for small businesses, typed resumes, did tax preparation, and translated court proceedings. The extra money earned from my side jobs made us some "fun money" to take our kids to different places when we weren't working.

Over time, and while still employed at the Assessor's office, the clothing business I operated from my car evolved into an actual boutique on Plaza Boulevard in National City. I brought in new stock regularly, and learned how to merchandise, budget, move inventory, and cut losses. I quickly realized what it meant to be a small business owner. I had overhead in the form of rent, employees, permits, insurance, and government reporting. Despite the headaches, stress, and time investment involved in operating a boutique, it was a valuable crash course on how to run a business and it gave me a greater appreciation for future ventures.

To diversify the boutique's inventory, I started selling a skincare product that was new on the market. I thought the product was great. I offered this business opportunity to select customers who wanted to earn some part-time income. I ended up having many agents who were doing outside sales. From this venture, I made an extra $5,000-10,000 a month. I supported my agents by holding marketing presentations for them, thereby growing the sales force. I learned a great deal about direct sales, training, and people in general. Secure in knowing that my parents and in-laws were providing the best care for our children, I was able to manage the boutique and my sales force, work at the Assessor's office, write commentaries for a local Filipino newspaper, and remain active in local organizations. I received invitations to speak at community events, including swearing-in ceremonies for new citizens. Little did I know then that those speeches would supplement my training for my future presentations in real estate.

As a result of hard work and multiple business ventures, we were able to buy a new four-bedroom home in San Diego, and we were able to meet our obligations comfortably.

We were living the American Dream.

Sort of, that is.

Although I owned the boutique, I wasn't necessarily making much more than when I was just selling part time from the trunk of my car. A lot of what was supposed to be our profit was spent on overhead. With the skincare business, I was making great money, but the company started having financial problems and abruptly closed. All the residuals I counted on to support my family disappeared in a flash. It was another huge setback. I felt badly for everyone on my sales team and the people in the company that I had befriended and worked with through the years. It was a hard lesson to learn, but it made me realize that if you are working for someone, you are at the mercy of whoever is at the top.

That hard lesson was repeated.

A developer was transforming a 100-acre rural RV park into a timeshare-like community designed to immerse families in Filipino cultural activities and events. My husband and I bought our membership and took our kids there on the weekends. Aside from enjoying activities like fishing, swimming, and horseback riding, they were also exposed to a piece of our culture.

Noting my dedication to the project, the owners soon offered me a full-time position as the marketing director for San Diego. After ten years of proudly serving the County of San Diego Assessor's Office, I quit so I could fully dedicate my time to making the venture a success.

As the owners began to develop the residences in phases, I sold memberships to people from all over the country. Unfortunately, memberships sold faster than the number of units being built and the owners were having a difficult time delivering their promised development on a timely manner. Not long after, many members grew frustrated, understandably so, and started complaining about the delay. Litigation followed and was later dismissed. Needless to say, there was just too much negative publicity for the project to rebound and it spiraled downward from there. I watched helplessly as a project I completely believed in—a venture that brought fun, camaraderie, and Filipino culture to our families—was dragged through the mud, until it eventually closed.

I was bitterly disappointed and remember it as one of the darkest periods in my life. Once again, we as a family were faced with tremendous uncertainty. Little did I know, I was getting closer than ever to where I wanted to be. Shortly after it closed, owners of a real estate company who'd read an article in the newspaper about the project's closure offered me a position as marketing director.

Weary after my previous experiences, I researched the company thoroughly and concluded the company was established, and offered a product that struck me as the most sensible: land.

I took the leap and agreed to become their marketing director.

After spending years dealing with other people's property, I now had the opportunity to help people become landowners. It was a challenge I enjoyed taking on. Given that it was a down market at the time, I had to build a sales force from scratch. I successfully recruited and trained some promising agents. I developed a presentation based on what I would want and need to know if I were the potential client. I then modified it based on my audience. My straightforward approach worked well in the U.S., despite market conditions at the time. I decided to take my land presentation overseas and focused on selling to business people abroad. The overseas market turned out to be healthy for us as well.

With my tenure at the Assessor's office, and now having gained in depth understanding and experience in real estate, I started to consider starting my own land company. As an immigrant, especially one who'd had enough prior setbacks to understand it took time, effort, money, hard work and even heartache to finally achieve what you want, I never thought that I could become a landowner in America.

Owning a land company seemed entirely out of the question.

It took a very scary, turbulent flight in the Philippines to shake up my thinking. As the small plane bucked up and down, and people screamed around me, I sat there praying to see my kids again. I also had a revelation about my career and the goals I'd set as a little girl, looking up at the same sky from which I was sure I would soon fall. I thought about what I wanted for myself and what I wanted to be able to provide not only for my family, but for other people as well. I wanted to live to embrace my children again and manifest the rest of my childhood dreams. The extreme turbulence eventually ceased and we landed at the airport, rattled but otherwise unharmed.

Shortly after the flight back home, I resigned from my position.

To my friends, including some family, I was making a grave mistake leaving the company where I worked. My decision was reminiscent of when I left my "stable" job with the county, unnecessarily giving up stability to start all over again. The mere idea was absurd to many of my loved ones.

While I've always believed that fateful Easter fire made it easier for me to adapt to whatever life threw at me, I was well aware that change could still be difficult. But, having gone through many rough patches in the past, I had become less and less afraid of taking chances. Somehow, each struggle made the next one easier to handle. Thankfully, my husband's full support and service in the Navy, coupled with my dad's unwavering faith in my ability to accomplish anything I put my mind to, gave me resolve and allowed me to take risks that would bring me closer to making my childhood dreams come to fruition.In 1999, I founded Capital Holdings.

My philosophy has remained the same since we started: I will only sell parcels I am willing to buy myself and I will always do my best to see from a client's perspective. I was certain that in order for both my company and my clients to thrive, I simply needed to understand where the next areas of development were likely to happen.

We all know how valuable land is, how it can benefit us in the future, and how we want it for ourselves and our children. But, like me, many people don't really understand where and how to buy land. Given what I have learned with research, time, and experience, I definitely know now that it is possible to own land on almost any budget. It may not always be feasible in already developed areas, but we do have a chance to own and afford land in upcoming and developing areas. Sharing this knowledge and opportunity with others is very rewarding. Giving others the opportunity to do the same is something that I absolutely enjoy doing.

Now you know my story. In *Owning Land Made Easy*, I look forward to helping you create the next great chapter in yours!

Jet Abuda-Sison

CHAPTER ONE

ROOTED IN THE LAND

L and is an integral part of our lives. It is the source of the food we eat, the foundation of the homes in which we live, the offices where we work, and the buildings where we manufacture the widgets we need. People's perception of its value may rise and fall depending on the state of the economy, but the need for land remains. In fact, as the population continues to increase (as it does even during recession), so does the demand for this finite necessity.

I quickly came to appreciate the crucial importance of land that Easter Sunday as a five-year-old when our house caught on fire. My family's only remaining possessions were the clothing on our backs, the little we scavenged from the charred remains, and what turned out to be one absolutely crucial asset—the land on which our house once stood.

With no homeowner's insurance at that time in the Philippines, my parents had no choice but to rebuild, literally post by post. As I slept in a house with a full view of the moon (due to a partially completed roof), I dreamt of the things I would someday buy and the places I would someday go to help support my family so they would never have to suffer ever again. While my plans included a successful career, multiple homes, fast cars, and living in other countries, I had no idea that the means to my end would be what was literally beneath my feet.

In the aftermath of the fire, our family's land provided more than just a spot to rebuild. We were also able to grow fruit and earn extra income by selling the excess harvest at a roadside stand. Most importantly, my parents were able to borrow against our property to rebuild our home and finance that which they valued most—education. Owning a piece of land ensured that my siblings and I were sent to the best schools, where we would graduate and attain the best education my parents could possibly afford.

My appreciation for land and its intrinsic value grew that much more. I did well in my studies and was accepted to a medical school in Manila. During my summer vacations in college, I worked full time in sales for prominent rental car companies and earned healthy commissions. Shortly after graduating from college, I married and migrated to the United States to put down new roots with my husband. Even though we were far away from home, I never forgot how the land my parents owned had provided so much for our family.

Immigrants and the Land

During my presentations, I will often ask people if they know someone who owns land and whether it has been beneficial to the owner. The answer is almost always a resounding *yes*. I'll also ask if they've met anyone who has regretted his decision to own land. Not only do they say *no*, but they also express regret that they haven't done the same. Attendees will often tell me stories about people in their country or hometown who own land and how they often turn out to be among the wealthiest and powerful citizens. Few people disagree that land is actually one of the safest places to invest your money.

There are a number of reasons why:

--Land is a universal commodity we can all understand, no matter where we are from.

--Land is a finite commodity.

--Land cannot be lost or stolen.

--Land requires minimal to no upkeep.

--Land continues to appreciate with time.

In my experience, immigrants often have a special awareness and appreciation of land for the following reasons:

Scarcity

The Philippines, where I am from, is a much smaller country with a larger population proportionate to its area than that of the United States. Available land is a scarce commodity. Land in Makati, Philippines, for instance, can be more expensive than land in downtown Los Angeles. Land values (as I see it) are often determined by population, not by whether the land is in a developing country or a rich country like America.

https://www.census.gov/population/international/data/idb/worldpopgraph.php

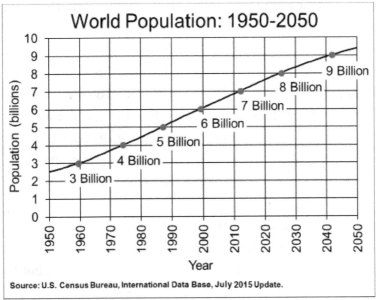

World Population Graph

The Importance of Land in Daily Life

In the Philippines for example, farming and agriculture are among the biggest industries, and an integral part of everyday existence for many families. Here in the U.S., farming is limited to a very few. I believe this difference makes immigrants more aware of the direct benefits of land.

Land is Everyone's First Love

As children we all loved playing in the dirt, on fields and playgrounds. My happiest memories from childhood involve playing with friends on playgrounds and out in the fields.

Pride of Ownership

Having come from another country, owning a piece of land in America gives us a sense of pride, belonging, and a permanent stake in our chosen country. The first thing that most immigrants want, and purchase as soon as they can afford it, is a home—a home, which, of course, sits on land.

Land Ownership in America Replaces Something Left Behind

As an immigrant, with children born here, land ownership allows us to create and nurture new roots. Owning land can give a full sense of ownership sooner and faster than home ownership, which usually comes with a steep price tag, a fifteen- to thirty-year mortgage, and a deed that belongs to the bank until the home is paid off.

Land is a Completely Understandable Commodity

I did not know much about the stock market, mutual funds, annuities, or other forms of investment when I first came here, but I certainly understood the value of land.

I believe that first-generation immigrants are amongst the hardest-working people. They have to be in order to adapt and survive in their chosen country. They rarely have time for much beyond providing for themselves and their families. Add in a language barrier to overcome, and cultural differences, and it makes sense that they would therefore prefer to focus on investments they already know and understand, like owning land.

Why then do so many immigrants like me often believe that owning land here in the United States will always be out of reach?

Like most people, I knew and understood the value of owning land, but when I saw "land for sale" signs in and around my adopted hometown of San Diego, California and called the numbers on the signs, I had immediate sticker shock. The properties were not only very expensive, but required cash or at least thirty percent down payment, and had short-term financing. For me, this halted any thoughts I had about acquiring land.

But only temporarily.

Those of us who are immigrants know that you leave your home country for the sake of your family. You do it so your children will have a better life and better opportunities. Most of us have to start over from scratch, and this usually comes with a lot of personal sacrifice. In the Philippines, I was training to be a doctor. When I came to the United States, the only job I could get was as a cashier at a gas station convenience store. Our first television set was a 12-inch black-and-white, lowest-priced model, because it was all Sears would loan us since we had no credit references. Our first car, a Chevy, was a stick shift, with no air conditioning and no FM radio. When I told my friends about the television I had and the car I drove in America, they would joke and tell me to check my map, because it sounded like I'd landed in a developing country, not America!

Luckily, my tenure at the gas station store was brief. Through hard work, education, and a few breaks, I was able to parlay one opportunity into the next. I gained experience in office work, marketing, corporate business, outside and retail sales, sometimes all at once. It wasn't until I landed a job at the San Diego Assessor's office that simply working for a paycheck intersected with my interest in, and ties to, the importance and value of land.

At the Assessor's office, I learned how real estate appraisals were done. I learned about assessed value, supplemental tax, how to read parcel maps, and much, much more. I also learned that people desire land and real estate here, just as they did in the Philippines. However, it was dispiriting to realize just how much land really cost in most urban areas. Even as a newly minted citizen of the United States, my desire to truly own property—not just pay a hefty mortgage to a bank—was tempered by a belief that land ownership was just for the very wealthy few.

I went on to get my real estate and broker's license. After selling vacation properties, I determined that residential real estate with its various mortgage restrictions wasn't for me. For instance, in my various readings, I've learned that only about twenty percent of the population can qualify for a mortgage because of the cost of improvement (i.e. the home) put on the land. With land, everybody can potentially be a client as there are companies like ours that requires little or no qualifying at all. The collateral is the land itself. Owning land made the most sense to me. Any investment is speculative, but owning land has historically proven to be one of the safest investments for a lot of people, and one I totally believed in and understood. Not only is it a good investment, it provides a good "Plan B" for people. If you are paying a mortgage on a home and you lose your job, or get sick and can no longer make your payments, it only takes three months before the bank starts to foreclose on you. If you own land, however, you can buy a trailer, park it there, and you have the peace of mind and security of knowing that whatever life throws at you, you have a place to go.

I began to realize that for most people, especially immigrants with limited resources, a family and its future prosperity to consider, parcels offered by land companies near where they live (which is normally in already well-developed cities) are just too costly. The other option is buying through land companies that typically acquire big pieces of land, subdivide them into smaller parcels, and sell them off to individual buyers. The availability of big parcels to subdivide usually means the land is far from cities or development, which may not always be what people are looking for. This business plan makes sense for most companies because it is easy to train agents who put all their marketing efforts on lots located in the same place. Busloads of people are brought in and adjoining lots are sold in the same subdivision. This makes touring efficient, because clients are only driven to one place instead of multiple locations.

Seeing this business model in action, I felt that companies were making clients cater to them instead of the other way around. Land being offered wasn't necessarily a good fit for a lot of potential buyers, especially those who might be looking to make a possible return on a shorter time frame.I began to ponder the possibilities of buying and selling more affordable land of different sizes in an area where growth appears to be imminent, but hasn't yet happened. Land would still be cheaper and affordable, but the chances of earning a healthy return would be even greater. Though this would entail buying and touring one parcel at a time, it could potentially be a win-win. In the long run, the clients would make more money and the company would earn the business of repeat customers and referrals.

With this in mind, I began to research various areas that had the most potential of becoming the next city, and where land was still cheap. Since the southern part of California has approximately 60 percent of the population in the state, and the population can only migrate eastward (since the Pacific Coast is to the west), I tracked the growth along the 15 Freeway from San Diego to Mira Mesa, Temecula, Murrieta, Corona, Ontario and Rancho Cucamonga. The busy 15 Freeway, widely considered the economic corridor in the west, is familiar to almost everyone as the route to Las Vegas. I saw this as a major advantage since people tend to be open to what they know and are already familiar with. As I researched the areas around the 15 Freeway, I realized how much was poised to happen growth-wise, and how little of the seemingly open space in San Bernardino County was actually available for sale.

One of the biggest eye-openers for me was learning from various sources that approximately 81 percent of the land in San Bernardino County, the largest county in California and the United States, is owned by the Federal Government and a little over two percent is owned by the State. Approximately four percent is owned by cement companies, and an additional four percent is owned by the railroad industry. This leaves little for developers to build on, or for cities to expand. The county appears to have large acreages up for grabs due to its vast desert landscapes, which alone can mislead people into believing land is widely available, thus perhaps worthless. However, approximately 91 percent of the land has been claimed. If you take away areas where roads are built or there are washes, mountains that can't be developed, existing commercial, residential and industrial developments, and parcels already owned by other investors and developers, there is actually a scarcity of available land. Seeing as value is derived by scarcity (like with diamonds and gold) wouldn't your perception of the land value change? Mine certainly did.

Land, like any other commodity, follows the basic law of supply and demand: the lower the supply, the higher the demand, and the higher the price.

I set my sights on Victor Valley, California, because of a number of factors which we will be covering in depth in a later chapter, including a new cargo airport designed to handle cargo flights coming into LAX, the influx of companies including General Electric, freeway infrastructure, availability of the California Aqueduct, the construction of a power plant, and the low cost of the land.

Capital Holdings

With my real estate experience and my tenure at the Assessor's office, I felt like I had an in-depth understanding of the business that I could use to benefit others. Using myself as a gauge for a client, I knew I could offer a better product. I founded Capital Holdings in 1999 with a plan to offer a better product and provide my clients with:

1. Affordable land in areas where precursors for growth are present
2. Locations where I believed my clients would make the most return
3. Customized parcels of various sizes and price points so my clients would have the opportunity to own land at a price they could truly afford
4. No qualifying requirement, and in-house financing
5. Offering only land that I myself was willing to buy

In order to create a win-win situation for our company and clients, I knew I would have to pick my location correctly and be aggressive on the buying end. I continued to do extensive and exhaustive research by walking and driving every inch of the Victor Valley and the surrounding areas. I studied whatever I could about the history and potential growth of the region, scoured any map we could get our hands on, and eventually learned the general topography. I met and befriended locals and attended city meetings. I started hanging out in the desert so much that we started to suspect that the squirrels and jackrabbits knew my scent!

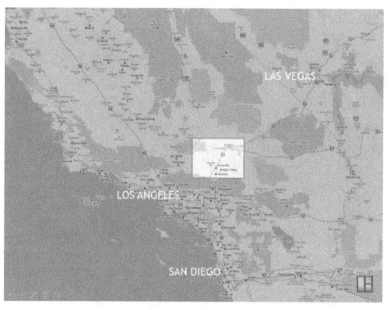

High desert nestled between the major cities of Los Angeles to the west, San Diego to the south, and Las Vegas to the east

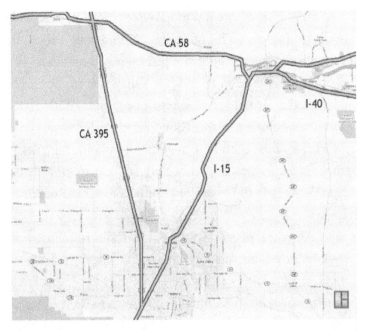

High desert between major arterial freeways of California State Route 395, Interstate 15, and California State Route 58

While I saw lots of potential, I also had to take into consideration the downsides of the area. George Air Force base had just closed at the time. The local residents, whom I spoke to and spent time with, were the most negative about the area's possibilities. People working in the city and county offices in the area were not much more encouraging. Nearly 10,000 jobs had just been lost with the base closure, so their attitudes were understandable. One broker went so far as to tell me that he'd feel bad if he didn't warn me that the area had sort of become a "meth lab," and that he questioned my sanity in wanting to buy up land in the area.

I thanked him, told him not to worry, and jokingly added, "I can only afford it while it's meth. Once it starts being a cocaine lab, the land around here is going to be too expensive for my budget."

When buying land, one has to have some foresight, especially if you're not working with a lot of capital. You must be willing to take risks, but your decision should not just be based on a leap of faith. My decision to buy land in the Victor Valley was supported by the knowledge of the area that I acquired over time. With affordable land, easy access along a major economic corridor, a cargo airport in the works, a plan to build a huge power plant, the presence of the California Aqueduct, and above all, still cheap land, I thought the Victor Valley had all the makings of becoming the next possible boom town.

I soon opened an office in Oceanside, California, just north of San Diego. I figured that, just because people like me couldn't afford to buy land in a populous area near where they lived, it didn't mean they weren't interested in owning land anywhere else. Since almost everyone is familiar with the Victor Valley, if only because they pass through the region on their way to Las Vegas, I felt confident that we'd invested in an ideal location.

Our clients, whom I urged to call land-for-sale signs in their area, quickly realized how expensive the land was around their neighborhoods. They then learned they could buy a $10,000 parcel of land in the Victor Valley with a $1,000 down payment and approximately $73 per month. All agreed it was a very affordable investment for people who could only afford to rent apartments. Once we brought them out to the Victor Valley for a tour and gave them an opportunity to own a 2.5-acre parcel for such a reasonable price, they were excited.

They were that much more excited when they realized how land gave them the ability to leverage. If you want to buy $10,000 of General Electric stocks, you need to have $10,000 to buy the stocks. And while most land companies do some financing, they will not do sales for as low as a 10 percent down payment and/or a big price reduction for cash. We did brisk business. We were able to turn parcels around quickly, and some were bought by developers for a very healthy profit. Capital Holdings quickly evolved from a dream into a bustling reality. As a result, we did a lot more sales than what we anticipated in our first year.

By 2000, we bought our first home office in the Victor Valley, and had established ourselves as a thriving local business in a community that was soon to be thriving once again. Not only did I now own land in my adopted home country, I was also able to make it possible for other people to see how easily they could become landowners too.

As a result of my success in land speculation, I was able to make my dream of providing homes for our parents a reality. One of those properties was a high-rise condo on the Las Vegas Strip. Although I purchased it at the peak of the market, and was well aware that it was not a good time to buy, I have no regrets. In fact, it turned out to be one of the best decisions I have ever made. We were watching fireworks on New Year's Day when my dad commented that he couldn't believe he would someday live on the Las Vegas Strip and be given the chance to enjoy the best fireworks, from the best view, ever. This memory gives me great joy. He passed away not long after.

It doesn't matter where one comes from; people are people and couldn't be any more the same. I find that we all share the same hopes, dreams, aspirations, and love of family. We all want happiness and financial security. While land is not for everybody, and I would never recommend putting all your eggs in one basket, it has been an important part of my investment portfolio and my life.

As my father used to say, cake tastes better when shared. If you try to eat it all by yourself, not only will you get fat, you will also get diabetes!

Allow me to offer you a slice of cake by showing you how owning land can work for you, too.

CHAPTER TWO

WHAT IS LAND SPECULATION?

One of the many reasons I decided to get into the land business is that people from every culture universally understand the concept of land. If I am selling a gadget, I have to show you how to use that particular thing and explain its value in your life. Everyone knows what land is, and understands it's where you grow food, build a home, construct buildings, and much more. For many immigrants like myself, land was the source of their family livelihood for generations. In my particular case, it was a place to go back to after our house burned to the ground, and an asset my parents could mortgage to rebuild and to educate us. Most people have a positive view of owning land and understand that it is actually one of the safest places to put your money.

Why is it then that most people hesitate, or don't invest in land at all, here in America?

I believe it is because of fear of the expense, and the lack of information about various aspects of speculative land investment.

I've learned over the years that the decision of owning land becomes much easier when people understand the *Whats, Whys, Wheres, Whens,* and *Hows* of owning land. At my in-person presentations at Capital Holdings, I make sharing the information I've learned and collected my main objective. I plan to do the same in this book.

Land is Speculative

Let's start with what some might consider the elephant in the room:

Yes, land is a speculative investment.

As with any investment, nobody can guarantee anything.

Keep in mind that putting money under your mattress can be speculative as well. You have no guarantee that it will always be there. Somebody can rob you of it. While putting your money in the bank may be the safest investment (up to what the FDIC will insure it for) the interest earned hardly even matches inflation. So, if there's any guarantee in putting your money in the bank, it is that it will lose value. I tell people that if you are honestly where you want to be in life already, there's no need to do anything more. But if you are not, you need to be open to looking at other possibilities.

Land, specifically **Land Banking**, can be one of them.

There's certainly more rhyme and reason to investing in land than there is in the stock market. Unlike many other types of investment, you can lessen the speculative aspect by doing your research. For instance, when I was looking for where to invest, I looked for areas where population was increasing, because increases in land value are directly based on population growth, not economics. For example, Orange County, California was once entirely rural. Had the population not increased, the land would not be worth what it is today. By attending public hearings, I learned where the freeways, railroads, utilities, and other infrastructure were to be built, and where large industrial companies were planning to build their facilities. I made my decisions about where to buy land accordingly.

Home Ownership

One of the biggest financial decisions we make in our lifetime is buying a home. When we purchased our first home, I was extremely proud to have our slice of the American pie. After all, what could be more important than owning your own home? It is where we live, have our families, raise and educate our children. In this country, we are sold on the idea of the American Dream: owning a house complete with a white picket fence. For this reason, we don't hesitate to allocate a third of our income, if not more, to this vitally important purchase.

Home sales drive the economy by affecting a lot of industries. Banks, real estate agents, cement companies, steel, glass, roofing, furniture, home decor, all benefit when you buy a home. People like the look of a new home with beautiful improvements inside and outside. Dirt is not as exciting, nor it would seem, as stimulating, to nearly as many industries.

But is it potentially a better investment than home ownership?

Many people believe buying a home is the same as owning land. For a long time, I was one of those people. That was, until I realized that, like all of us, I was only three missed mortgage payments away from the bank initiating the process of taking back the property. Nevertheless, my husband and I made pretty good equity on our home, and I was happy for that, even if at that time I did not totally understand the process. I was also one of those who believed the common misconception that it was *my* house that was mostly "going up" in value.

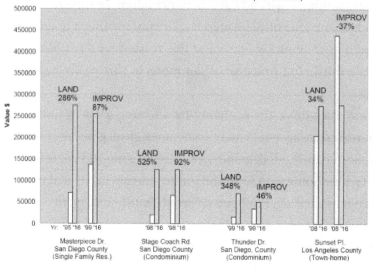

Examples of County Assessed Values Over A Period of Time
(With Percent Increase of Land vs. Improvements)

*County Assessed Values do not always reflect market values. Figures do not reflect homeowners exemption.

EXAMPLES OF COUNTY ASSSED VALUES OVER A PERIOD OF TIME
(LAND vs. IMPROVEMENTS)

Masterpiece Drive, San Diego, CA 92057 (Single Family Residence)				
		Land Value		Improvements Value
1995	$	71,185.00	$	136,559.00
2016	$	275,000.00	$	255,000.00
% Change from 1995 to 2016		286%		87%

Stage Coach Rd, San Diego, CA 92057 (Condominium)				
		Land Value		Improvements Value
1998	$	20,000.00	$	65,100.00
2002	$	28,111.00	$	78,716.00
2016	$	125,000.00	$	125,000.00
% Change from 1998 to 2016		525%		92%

Thunder Drive, San Diego, CA 92056 (Condominium)				
		Land Value		Improvements Value
1999	$	15,583.00	$	34,075.00
2002	$	16,535.00	$	36,160.00
2016	$	69,800.00	$	49,855.00
% Change from 1999 to 2016		348%		46%

Sunset Place, Diamond Bar, CA 91765 (Townhome)				
		Land Value		Improvements Value
2008	$	204,000.00	$	437,706.00
2016	$	273,811.00	$	275,975.00
% Change from 2008 to 2016		34%		-37%

*County assessed values are not always market values.

The chart and graph above show four examples of different types of properties I purchased in the past. It shows that based on the respective counties' assessments, land increased several times more than the increase (or decrease) of improvements. As I found out, and as shown on the chart below using some of the homes we've previously owned, the substantial increase in value is on the land, and not on the house itself.

My general observation is that beyond the cyclical lows of real estate, the overall trend in value is that land continues to increase over a long period of time. In addition, and based on my personal purchases, I have found that land values increase at a rate faster than improvements (i.e. house structure). Homes do get older, outdated, and can lose some of their value depending on the work that needs to be done. The land below them however, almost never changes—except to become scarce in a particular area and, usually, more valuable.

We all grow up being told that buying a house will bring us security, happiness, comfort, and that it is a great investment. While a change in thinking, especially about your home, can be difficult, scary, and even uncomfortable, consider this: ten percent per year in appreciation, or anything way higher than inflation, seems to not be sustainable. This may very well be one of the reasons the market crashed in 2008. Therefore, houses should probably only increase in value by three to five percent per year (but this is just a bit higher than inflation). If your asset is only increasing by three to five percent per year, and inflation is almost at the same rate, is this really the most sensible place to invest all your money? Shouldn't you diversify your investment portfolio?

While we all need somewhere to call home, I found myself wondering if I actually needed to be a "homeowner"? At one time, I was paying almost $3,000 a month for a home I'd purchased for about $300,000. The loan was for thirty long years. A mentor of mine explained that I would likely not pay the house off in my lifetime, as I would most likely borrow against it in emergencies and when the kids needed it for school, just like my parents had done with their land after the fire. He suggested that I could sell our house and maybe rent or get a lease with option to purchase a similar home in and around the same neighborhood. Our monthly payment would likely fall to half, maybe $1,500 a month. In turn, I should use the $1,500 I was saving every month to buy three pieces of land at $500 a month each in a developing area. If I chose my locations wisely, one of the three lots had a good chance of appreciating to $300,000 in five to ten years. I would then be able to purchase a home for cash and still have two parcels to use for retirement.

It was one of the best bits of advice I ever received.

Commonly used Terms and Concepts in Real Estate

While I would never advocate selling your house and using the proceeds to invest in land unless you've thoroughly researched the idea, understand your budget, and have thought out every conceivable detail first, I would urge you to know and understand the following ten concepts and answers to questions regarding real estate:

1. Property Tax

"Property tax is a tax based on the value of a house or other property. A property tax bill includes a variety of different taxes and charges. In California, a property tax bill includes the one percent rate, voter-approved debt rates, parcel taxes, Mello-Roos taxes, and assessments. The taxes due from the one percent rate and voter-approved debt rates are based on a property's assessed value.

The California Constitution sets the process for determining a property's taxable value. Although there are some exceptions, a property's assessed value typically is equal to its purchase price, adjusted upward each year by two percent. Under the constitution, other taxes and charges may not be based on the property's value."

Source: http://www.lao.ca.gov/
reports/2012/tax/property-tax-primer-112912.aspx

2. Tax Assessment

"The tax assessment is the value given to property that is being taxed. Multiplying the net taxable valuation by the tax rate yields the tax due."

Source: http://www.sco.ca.gov/
ardtax_ctcrefman_glossary.html#T

3. Mello-Roos

"In 1982, the Mello-Roos Community Facilities Act of 1982 (Government Code Section 53311-53368.3) was created to provide an alternate method for financing needed improvements and services to local public agencies. The Act allows any county, city, special district, school district or joint powers authority to establish a Mello-Roos Community Facilities District (a "CFD"), which allows for financing of public improvements and services. The services and improvements that Mello-Roos CFDs can finance include streets, sewer systems, and other basic infrastructure, police protection, fire protection, ambulance services, schools, parks, libraries, museums and other cultural facilities. By law, the CFD is also entitled to recover expenses needed to form the CFD and administer the annual special taxes and bonded debt."

Source: http://www.californiataxdata.com/pdf/Mello-Roos2.pdf

4. Proposition 8

"In 1978, California voters passed Proposition 8, a constitutional amendment to Article XIII A that allows a temporary reduction in assessed value when real property suffers a decline in value. A decline in value occurs when the current market value of real property is less than the current assessed (taxable) factored base year value as of the lien date, January 1. Proposition 8 is codified by section 51(a)(2) of the Revenue and Taxation Code."

Source: http://www.boe.ca.gov/proptaxes/faqs/prop8.htm#1

5. When does Assessed Value change?

"A property's assessed value changes when there is a change in ownership or new construction. This assessed value is typically the sales price, but the final assessed value is determined by the county assessor. The assessed value can also change and be reassessed temporarily (Proposition 8) when the market values have declined.

Real property may decline in market value from one lien date to the next lien date; however, it will not benefit from a lower assessment unless its market value falls below the current factored base year value. For example, if you purchase your property during a time when the real estate market falls dramatically, or if your property is substantially damaged due to a storm or fire that causes a reduction in your property's value, it is likely that your property will benefit from a Proposition 8 reassessment. The decline in value is typically temporary and may be the result of changes in the real estate market, the neighborhood, or the property itself.

When the market value of a property on the January 1 lien date falls below the factored base year value (assessed value), the assessor is obligated to review the property and enroll the lesser of the factored base year value or market value. The factored base year value of real property is the market value as established in 1975 or as established when the property last changed ownership or when the property was newly constructed.

A property that has been reassessed under Proposition 8 is then reviewed annually to determine its lien date value. The assessed value of a property with a Proposition 8 value in place may increase each lien date (January 1) by more than the standard two percent maximum allowed for properties assessed under Proposition 13; however, unless there is a change in ownership or new construction, a property's assessed value can never increase above its factored Proposition 13 base year value after adjusting for the annual increase.

This review process is performed by the county assessor and is in addition to the formal appeal process with the county assessment appeals board that is available to taxpayers. Some counties provide an application for "Decline in Value" reassessment. Owners should contact their counties, as they may have different procedures."

Source: http://www.boe.ca.gov/proptaxes/faqs/prop8.htm#1

6. How does Escrow work?

"Escrow is the process whereby parties to the transfer of financing of real estate deposit documents, funds, or other things of value with a neutral and disinterested third party (the escrow agent), which are held in trust until a specific event or condition takes place according to specific, mutual written instructions from the parties. Escrow is essentially a clearinghouse for the receipt, exchange, and distribution of the items needed to transfer or finance real estate. When the event occurs or the condition is satisfied, a distribution or transfer takes place. When all the elements necessary to consummate the real estate transactions have occurred, the escrow is "closed". "

Source: http://www.dre.ca.gov/
files/pdf/Escrow_Info_Consumers.pdf; page 5

7. What is a Title?

"Title in real estate indicates "fee" position of lawful ownership and right to property. It is the "bundle of rights" possessed by an owner. It is the combination of all elements constituting proof of ownership."

Source: http://www.sco.ca.gov/
ardtax_ctcrefman_glossary.html#M

8. What is a Deed of Trust?

"A Deed of Trust is the legal document by which a borrower pledges certain real property as a guarantee for the repayment of a loan. A Deed of Trust differs from a mortgage in some important respects. For example, instead of two parties to the transaction, there are three: 1) the borrower, or trustor, who signs the trust deed; 2) the third or neutral party, the trustee, to whom the trustor deeds the property as security for payment of the debt; and 3) the lender, or beneficiary, who benefits from the pledge agreement. In the event of a default, the trustee can sell the property and transfer the money thus obtained to the lender as payment of the debt."

Source: http://www.sco.ca.gov/

9. What is Reconveyance?

"Reconveyance is the transfer of the title of land from one person to the immediately preceding owner. This instrument of transfer is commonly used to transfer the legal title from the trustee to the trustor (borrower) after a trust deed debt has been paid in full."

Source: http://www.sco.ca.gov/
ardtax_ctcrefman_glossary.html#M

10. When is property tax due?

For the County of San Bernardino, California, the fiscal year for property taxes runs from July 1 to June 30 of the following year. The annual tax bill is divided into two installments, the first due on or before December 10, and the second due on or before April 10. The first installment covers taxes for the first six months of the fiscal tax year from July 1 to December 31. The second installment covers the next six months from January 1 to June 30. Property owners also have the option to pay the full annual amount on or before December 10.

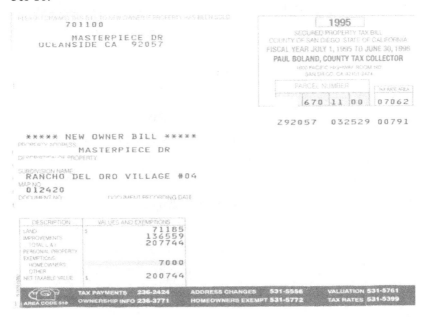

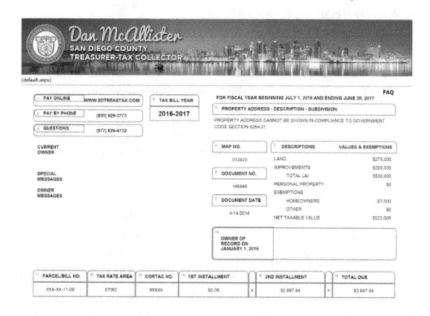

At the time of purchase, property taxes are prorated between the seller and buyer based on the recorded date of the grant deed (usually done in escrow). If you purchased your property and closed escrow on October 1, for example, you will be responsible for the last three months of the first installment bill which will cover October 1 to December 31. Therefore, you would be prorated for half of the first installment amount due. This is usually charged to you at the closing of escrow. You are then responsible for payments of the second and future installments thereafter.

Speculative Land Sales: a whole other language

If you've bought a house, you know the drill with real estate agents, commissions, etc. The learning curve involved in land sales may seem even more complex, but that's only because it's a new concept to most of us.

At Capital Holdings, I present potential clients with as much in-formation as I can about land. I think it is crucial that they fill in whatever gaps they have in their knowledge, from how land is sub-divided to issues involved in zoning. I am constantly amazed by how helping them understand as much as possible about land, and pur-chasing speculative land, helps aid them in their decision-making process. When it comes to understanding land, nothing is too ba-sic. When a client isn't originally from the U.S., answers to questions like how many feet are in a mile (5,280) or how many acres are in a hectare (2.47105) can be very important, because a lot of countries use the metric system, while here land is measured in linear square feet. This fact alone is an eye-opener for many, as are the maps we've acquired through various sources. Before I show anyone an actual parcel or even do a Google tour of a property, we look at flat maps for reference, topographical maps to show elevation, and aerial maps that show a particular parcel in relation to the nearest city, airport, and other landmarks.

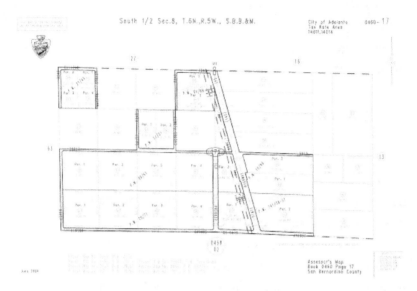

South 1/2 Sec.8, T.5N.,R.5W., S.B.B.&M.

City of Adelanto
Tax Rate Area
14011,14018

0460- 17

Assessor's Map
Book 0460 Page 17
San Bernardino County

Sample of an Assessor's Parcel Map

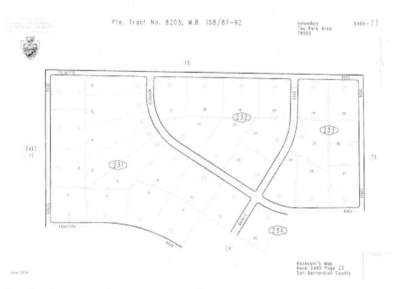

Ptn. Tract No. 8203, M.B. 108/87-92

Helendale
Tax Rate Area
36005

0485- 23

Assessor's Map
Book 0485 Page 23
San Bernardino County

Sample of an Assessor's Tract Map my real estate agents show clients before taking them on a tour of a property of interest.

When prospective clients come into my office for a presentation, I make sure they know the answers to important questions like:

What makes up a section of land?

"A section is a unit of land established by government survey that contains 640 acres. It is one mile square with 36 sections making up one survey township on a rectangular grid."

Source: http://www.sco.ca.gov/
ardtax_ctcrefman_glossary.html#T

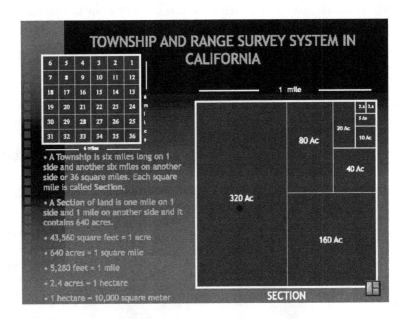

What makes up a township?

"A township in the United States is a small geographic area. In the survey of public lands of the United States, a territorial subdivision six miles long and six miles wide, containing 36 one-mile-square sections, located between two range lines and two township lines."

Source: http://www.sco.ca.gov/
ardtax_ctcrefman_glossary.html#T

How do you physically locate a specific parcel?

Each section (one square mile) usually has a corner monument (see picture below), located on each corner indicating the township, range and section numbers. A lot of people have not seen one, and find it fascinating when we show it on some of our tours. Another way to locate a specific parcel is by using different types of maps, a Thomas Guide, or GPS, which I find to be very helpful and easy to use. We can normally drive or walk to the approximate general location of the land, but for those who want the exact location of a parcel, we recommend a licensed surveyor.

Corner Monument

How big is the lot for a standard home?

"The median average lot size in the USA is 8,750 square feet. The average home itself in America is 2,330 square feet. Lot dimensions have actually gone down from 10,125 square feet in 1976. What is increasing is the demand for larger houses."

Source: http://www.dimensionsinfo.com/average-lot-size-in-usa/

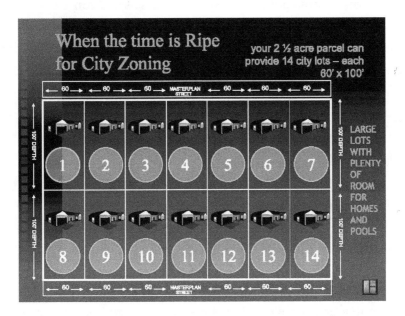

How are freeway exits tied in to how we divide our land?

Major freeway exits, depending on the topography, are normally found on section lines. As the city grows, exits are usually located on the half section, ¾ section and ¼ section.

Once I'm certain a prospective client has a good grasp of the above terms and other relevant pieces of information, I'll show them how to read an assessor's parcel map, including how the parcel numbers are derived, how it relates to a city zoning map, and the various zoning requirements.

I go into this much detail so people can not only understand and appreciate the potential value of prospective properties I offer, but opportunities all around them.

For instance, most people are annoyed when they become stuck in traffic due to road construction. Rather than being upset, I say why not see it as a possible opportunity instead? We do not widen our roads here in America just because we are bored, or have nothing to do with our tax dollars. When I find myself in a construction-related traffic jam, I see it as an indicator that I may be driving through the next area poised for growth because of a population increase that created the need for wider roads or more services. I take it as a sign that I should look into the cost of land in the area. Or, better yet, the path of development just beyond that location. An area can only take so much congestion before people and companies start looking for the next viable location.

I honestly believe that basic and useful information about land, or real estate in general, needs to be taught in school. Buying real estate is one of the biggest and most impactful purchases we will make in our lifetime. I find that tying it in to everyday life not only makes sense, but makes land, a topic I already find fascinating, that much more interesting.

To that end, I have included the following additional questions, information, and points of reference for you to learn and consider.

1. What are zoning requirements?

"Areas of land are divided by appropriate authorities into zones, within which various uses are permitted. Zoning ordinances and regulations are laws setting limits on how you can use your property. Cities, counties, townships and other local governments use zoning laws to guide development and shape the community, usually under an overall zoning plan."

> Source: http://zoning-planning-land-use.lawyers.com/
> zoning-ordinances-and-regulations.html

Below are examples of City General Plan Land Use and Zoning Maps:

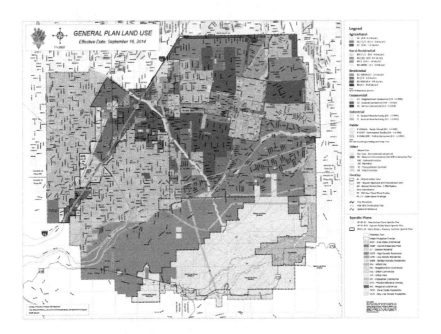

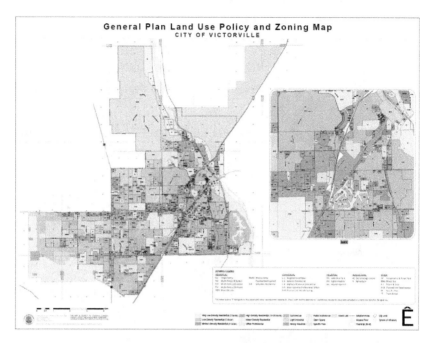

General Plan Land Use Policy and Zoning Map
CITY OF VICTORVILLE

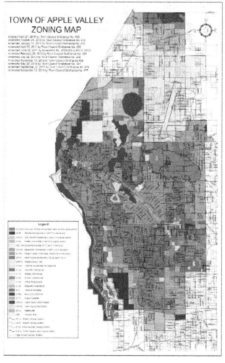

TOWN OF APPLE VALLEY
ZONING MAP

2. What is the significance of buying on a section line within a square mile?

"Section lines tend to be where the major exits are, and will therefore be wider, bigger streets that are more travelled. Land in this area offers a better chance of allowing commercial use."

Source: http://zoning-planning-land-use.lawyers.com
/zoning-ordinances-and-regulations.html

3. Land Pricing

Land is sold for whatever the buyer is willing to pay and the seller is willing to sell. In my experience, if a builder is making an acquisition and needs your parcel to complete whatever acreage they need to obtain, they will normally pay what the seller is asking.

4. How many homes can you build in an acre?

Depending on what the city requires of an area, 2.5 acres or more may be required for a home in low-density areas, to as small as 3,000 square feet for a home in a high-density area.

5. What are the different zonings for land?

Here are some of the major types of zoning in the U.S. that we normally deal with:

Residential: Residential zoning is for individual family units or groups. It includes single-family homes, duplexes, condominiums, trailer parks, and apartments. If the building you want to use for your business is zoned "residential," you will need to get a variance to use the property for business purposes.

Commercial : Commercial property includes almost everything that is not residential, from offices to retail stores, to shopping malls and strip malls, to bars and nightclubs. Most professional offices are zoned commercial.

Industrial: Industrial zoning is for manufacturing and warehousing operations.

Agricultural: Agricultural zoning is generally used by communities that are concerned about maintaining the economic viability of their agricultural industry. Agricultural zoning typically limits the density of development and restricts non-farm uses of the land. In many agricultural zoning ordinances, the density is controlled by setting a large minimum lot size for a residential structure. Densities may vary depending upon the type of agricultural operation. Agricultural zoning can protect farming communities from becoming fragmented by residential development. In many states, agricultural zoning is necessary for federal voluntary incentive programs, subsidy programs, and programs that provide for additional tax abatements.

Rural: The "rural" zoning designation is often used for farms or ranches. In certain parts of the country, this designation will include residences zoned to allow horses or cattle.

Combination: Any number of zoning designations can be combined to form some sort of combination zone, many of which are unique to the community adopting the particular designation."

Source: http://biztaxlaw.about.com/od/glossaryz/g/zoning.htm
Source: http://realestate.findlaw.com/land-use-laws/types-of-zoning.html

CHAPTER THREE

WHY LAND?

There is no denying that land literally provides the basis of life. Given that we depend on land for food, shelter, and every resource we mine from or develop upon it, land is also the source of all wealth. By its very nature, the value of land in our lives, and its impact on our future, is innately understandable.

Land:
--Cannot be lost or stolen
--Requires little upkeep (with the exception of some weed and trash abatements)
--Can provide financial freedom
--Can be an investment for our children's education
--Can be a valuable inheritance
--Can provide a tax deferral
--Can be a personal tax deduction

Speculative Land Buying
Buying land is not for everybody, and I am in no way going to urge you to invest all your money in any one thing. Land, however, can be a solid and profitable addition to anybody's investment portfolio. I do not recommend buying land if you are looking to flip the

property immediately. Just like the stock market, it is better to consider yourself in it for the long term. While land must be looked at as a long-term investment, if you buy in an area where precursors for growth are present (which we'll be discussing in depth in the next chapter), the time frame for earning a healthy profit can and does shorten significantly.

I personally believe in, and have profited from, buying land. Not only is it the source of all wealth, it is the best form of speculative investment for a variety of reasons:

1. Land is a tangible commodity.

Over the years, I have discovered that many immigrants harbor doubts about the banking system, not to mention the stock market, often due to lack of knowledge or unfamiliarity. It is not unheard of, even in this day and age, for banks in some countries to close and leave the depositors hanging. Banking in other countries is not as regulated as it is here in the U.S. As a result, it is not uncommon for my foreign-born clients to bring in cash—and by cash, I don't mean a check or cashier's check—to pay their down payments. I have been paid with bills kept in a shoebox, lunch box, or paper bags. I can therefore attest to the fact that there are still those who keep money underneath their mattresses where they can see and easily access it. For those people, land they can see, touch, and step upon is an understandable, logical, tangible commodity where they can safely "save" their money.

2. You can't control stocks, but you do have some control where land is concerned.

The old real estate adage "location, location, location" couldn't be more accurate. Like most investments, the value of land increases over time and investors can get in at any point. If you buy land in an area of growth, you have made a safe and appreciating investment. In addition, you can often control the value of land by developing the parcel for commercial, residential, and, in some cases, other uses such as a solar lease.

3. You can leverage your money.
Not only can you leverage your money by buying land, you can do so affordably. If you want to buy $10,000 in stocks, you need to have $10,000 cash to purchase the stocks. With land, you can buy a $10,000 piece of land for a $1,000 down payment and $72.42 payment monthly (based on a thirty-year term at 9 percent interest). This provides an affordable way for people with limited disposable income to invest in an appreciating asset.

4. You need not be a citizen or resident of the U.S. to purchase land.
Unlike some other countries, neither citizenship nor even residency is required to be a landowner in the United States.

5. There is no qualifying necessary.
With homes, one has to qualify because of the cost of improvement that's been put on the land. With undeveloped land, there's no need for the buyer to qualify because the collateral is the land itself. This creates a much bigger market where almost everyone can own land.

So, why bank on something like land? If you're looking for a stable, secured, long-term investment with near limitless potential, then why not?

Why I Sell Land
There was a point in time when I was debating whether to become a residential real estate broker, a commercial broker, or focus solely on

land. Once I compared the possibilities side by side, the answer was obvious. With home sales, the market can only be approximately 20 percent of the population, because buying a home requires a larger down payment, a certain credit score, and a variety of other qualifying factors to secure a loan. With land, it is possible for almost everyone to be a client. By buying and selling land, I can offer a small house lot to somebody who just wants to build a home, a bigger parcel to someone who someday wants to have a farm, or even 160 acres for someone with plans to build a theme park.

When I do a presentation for a prospective client, I usually ask that person, or couple, to bring along everyone who will be part of the decision-making process. I encourage people to bring their spouse, children, accountant, financial advisor, mailman—whomever they will be consulting so they can understand and answer the all-important question: *Why land?*

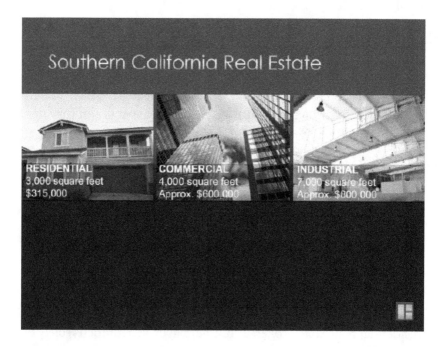

Southern California Real Estate

VACANT LOT
13 Acres (566,280 square feet)
Approx. $175,000

Southern California Real Estate

- Tenant management
- Building upkeep & maintenance
- Disasters (natural or man-made)
Subjected to high risk for profit loss

+ Acquisition of larger acreage
+ Virtually zero physical upkeep
+ Withstand disasters (natural or man-made)
Greater profit margin & potential

Other Real Estate vs Vacant Land

In comparison to other real estate ventures out there, why land?

For the same amount of money it costs to purchase a residential unit, commercial office space, or an entire industrial facility, you can instead own a larger space in land, which in turn increases your profit potential.

Land will always be there during your lifetime. While the sands may shift, the boundaries are always there. It also handles itself, withstanding disasters (such as fires, earthquakes, etc.) on its own, regardless of where you are in this world.

As I've mentioned, we do a thorough, educational presentation at Capital Holdings where we strive to answer any and all possible concerns. The people closest to the client will normally be the first folks they speak with after a presentation. If they are not there, they will shoot the idea down and create fear, not necessarily because they don't want their friend or family member to own land, but because it is just the normal precautionary thing you do for a loved one who is making an impactful financial decision—particularly given most people's preconceived notions that land is expensive, will require a 30 percent down payment, and is simply out of reach for "regular" folks.

Parents who have adult children will often tell me it is like pulling teeth to get their kids to agree to come along for the presentation. It is easy to understand why. Not only is it not their idea to spend what they expect will be a dull morning or afternoon learning about land, but there is also a lack of familiarity. Never mind the concerns they have about what their parents may be getting themselves into. While the topic admittedly does sound boring, the opportunities offered by land are anything but dull. Once the "support staff" is here, however, they are usually the ones that get the most excited about owning land. It is not at all uncommon to set up a presentation for a couple and have everybody else in attendance buy a parcel, too.

This confirms what I've learned and know about land ownership: pretty much everybody is open to the idea once they understand the value and how easily it works. A lot of people, especially young adults, have an extra $150 a month. They simply do not know (or haven't been given a good idea) where to put it. If they are not in a position when they come in for the presentation, I find they often come back in a year or years later wanting to speculate in land when they do have the available funds.

Why land is a good investment

I started Capital Holdings in 1999 by driving around the Victor Valley, learning everything I could about the area. Once I was certain this was the area I wanted to focus on, and that it would make the best sense for the company and our clients, I did all the due diligence I possibly could. Once I was satisfied with my research, I started buying properties one at a time, all of which were properties that I was willing to own myself.

I offer clients the opportunity to own land with as low as a 10 percent down payment and up to thirty-year terms with no prepayment penalty. Carrying the note for up to thirty years makes it possible for a lot of people, because it lowers their monthly payment. This provides Capital Holdings monthly receivables—a benefit that has served both the company and our clients for the past seventeen years.

Many of our clients have received offers on their land in two, five, or ten years. They have sold their parcels for a substantial profit. Others, like one client who received a two million dollar offer on her parcel, have refused to sell. When a client does decide to sell and pays off his account with us, we do our best to keep track of the buy and sell prices.

Below are some graphs with samples of offers and resale transactions. These are just samples of the transactions of offers and resale that happened with our knowledge. Some offers and resells occur outside of Capital Holdings, Inc.

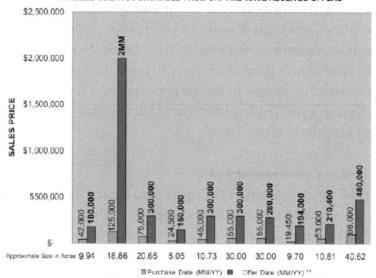

PARCELS CLIENTS PURCHASED FROM CHI* AND HAVE RECEIVED OFFERS

Approximate Size in Acres: 9.94 18.86 20.65 5.05 10.73 30.00 30.00 9.70 10.81 40.62

■ Purchase Date (MM/YY)   ■ Offer Date (MM/YY) **

* CHI = Capital Holdings, Inc. and/or its affiliates
** Offer Date is based the date reference on the letter of intent/offer. Figures above reflect samples
   of top known transactions of parcels that have received letter(s) of intent and/or offer(s).
   Past performances do not guarantee future results. All investments involve different degree of risk.

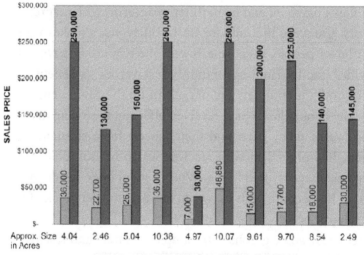

PARCELS CLIENTS PURCHASED FROM CHI* AND RESOLD FOR PROFIT

Approx. Size in Acres: 4.04 2.46 5.04 10.38 4.97 10.07 9.61 9.70 8.54 2.49

■ Purchase Date (MM/YY)   ■ Resold Date (MM/YY) **

* CHI = Capital Holdings, Inc. and/or its affiliates
** Resold Date is based on recorded date on grant deed or close of escrow date.
   Figures above reflect samples of top known transactions. Past performances do not guarantee
   future results. All investments involve different degree of risk.

Nothing delights me more than having a client pay off a loan because he or she has resold the land for a substantial profit, especially when they purchased the land from us for 10 percent down payment, and have only been paying $100 or $200 a month.

People ask me all the time if I wish I'd just held on to some of the land myself. The answer is, I don't. That's simply not my philosophy. Clients make money with us because they depend on our ability to speculate where land will most likely appreciate. When clients make money, they often buy again, and refer new customers.

Calling to inform clients about an offer on their parcel is one of the best perks of the job. It makes me happy that the success of our business provides income for our clients, and our employees, agents, contractors, and architects. It makes me even happier when clients call and thank us for the opportunities that land ownership has afforded them. Honestly, there's nothing quite as satisfying as an all-around win-win!

CHAPTER FOUR

WHERE TO BUY LAND

Growing up in another country has made me greatly appreciative of my daily life as an American. When I hear people complain about any aspect of the American government, I can't help but be reminded of people in other countries. I only wish that other governments had the stability of the United States. I believe everyone should experience life in another country so that they don't take ours for granted. No form of government is perfect, but the United States works diligently with its people to try and make things right. We have freedom of speech, suffrage, and a justice system that aims for just outcomes.

I once had the privilege of being sued. I say "privilege" because it taught me so many things. Looking back, and having gone through a lawsuit, it made me realize that anybody can sue you or call you names, but as long as you do things you know are right, and do what is within the law, you have nothing to worry about beyond your legal fees.

There are intelligent, hard-working people throughout the world that simply aren't given the same opportunities that we, as citizens, have to succeed. Here in America, we have the ability to choose our careers, invest in our own future, and partake in the progression of our nation.

As a strong believer in this country and a strong believer in land, it stands to reason that I chose (and continue to choose) to invest here in the United States. That said, I do not make financial decisions based on emotion or patriotism alone. I also make decisions based on dollars and sensibility.

In this chapter, we will look at the various facts and figures that compelled me to put my money into American real estate, and the parameters I used to determine the location that suited both my economic and financial goals. I believe my process can be applied to buying land anywhere.

Let's start with the big picture:

Where in the World?

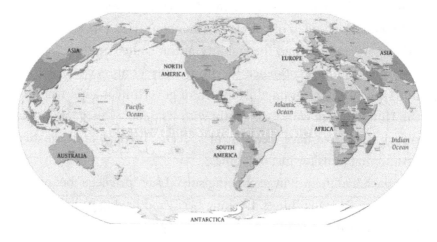

First and foremost, you need to determine where you want to own land. Land is an available commodity and a worthy investment across many countries. It can be less expensive in other places, but there may be restrictions as to who can own it. I chose to invest in the United States for the following reasons:

1. The United States has the world's largest economy. According to CNN Money, the Gross Domestic Product of the United States

was 19.0 trillion dollars. China is a distant second at 12.0 trillion dollars.

2. The U.S. population has grown from 152.2714 million in July of 1950 to 321.4188 million in July 2015. Our population is estimated to grow to 438 million by 2050.

Source: https://www.google.com/publicdata/
explore?ds=kf7tgg1uo9ude_

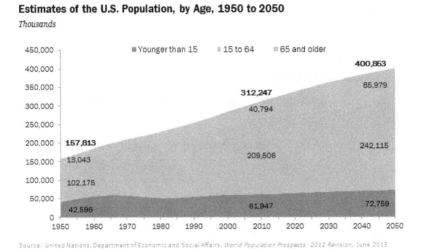

Estimates of the U.S. Population, by Age, 1950 to 2050

Pew Research Center Estimates of U.S. Population by Age

3. Citizenship is not a requirement in land ownership.

4. As a naturalized United States citizen, with children born in this country, buying land in America made the most sense for my family and their future.

Where in the United States?

As we know, the United States is a large country of varied terrain that consists of urban and rural areas, cities with different characteristics, demographics, weather, and real estate markets. Having lived in

Connecticut, I experienced the harsh winters of the East Coast and had little inclination to reside and/or buy land there. Everyone has preferences, but as someone born and raised in the tropics, the harsh winters were simply not for me. As soon as we moved to California, I fell in love with the beautiful weather and its diverse cultural appeal. I knew then that I'd found the place where I wanted to live, and invest in my future.

I considered buying land in other states where the weather was also appealing and the land was affordable, but California remained the ideal state for me.

Here is why:

• California has grown from 10.677 million in July 1950, to the most populous state in the nation with 39.1448 million in July 2015.

Source: https://www.google.com/publicdata/
explore?ds=kf7tgg1uo9ude_

• The population is projected to reach 50 million by 2049 via birth, immigration, and migration.

• Every sixth baby in the U.S. is born in California.

• According to recent figures released by Governor Jerry Brown's administration and based on data from the International Monetary Fund and the U.S. Bureau of Economic Analysis, California ranks just behind France and Brazil as the sixth largest economy in the world!

• California is the nation's gateway to the multibillion-dollar Pacific Rim Market, which grows by the millions each year and leads the nation in foreign investment transactions.

• Approximately 210,000 jobs are created in California each year.

- California is home to one of the best and most enduring real estate markets in the country.
- California boasts a progressive business climate.
- There is great weather, year round.
- California is one of the very best recreational destinations in the world.

California has experienced rapid population growth

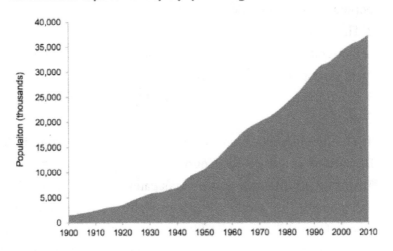

Sources: California Department of Finance estimates; U.S. Census Bureau estimates.

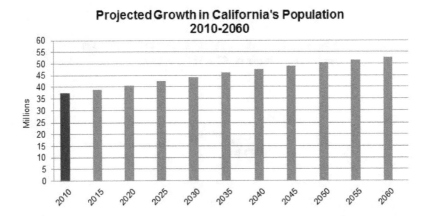

After deciding that California was the best state for me to invest in, I had to decide which region to focus on. As a resident of the San Diego area, my familiarity combined with the easy accessibility to land in the area pointed toward Southern California. I researched the economy and demographics of Southern California and learned the following:

1. Southern California is home to nearly 60 percent of the state's population (22.68 million in 2010).

2. There has been explosive growth due to birthrate, immigration, and migration, which has resulted in numerous stages of development throughout Southern California.

3. Continued growth in Los Angeles, Orange County, San Diego County.

4. The development boom in the Inland Empire located in San Bernardino and Riverside Counties.

5. Southern California is America's gateway to the multibillion-dollar Pacific Rim Market, which grows by the millions each year. Goods from Asia are most likely to enter the U.S. through the ports in Los Angeles and Long Beach en route to the rest of the country.

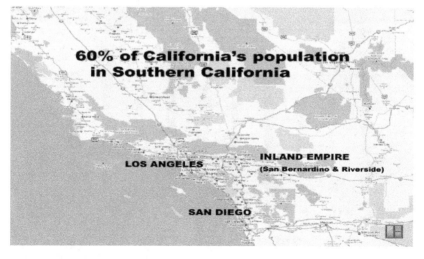

As I've mentioned, I initially thought that owning land in America would be impossible, especially in Southern California. I used to call phone numbers posted on land-for-sale signs in and around San Diego and get a serious case of sticker shock. Not only was the land very expensive, but the terms—a 30 percent or more down payment or a cash-only option—were impossible for me to meet. For most people, this could mean the end of their pursuit of the dream of owning land, but I was determined to somehow make it happen.

I knew I could not afford, nor compete, with established developers or investors with way deeper pockets than I could ever hope to have. However, some of the greatest fortunes in land were made in regions just outside of, or easily accessible to, the metropolitan areas like Los Angeles. Roy Sakioka and the Irvine family made fortunes from their land in Orange County. Bob Hope made a fortune by investing in Palm Springs, Howard Hughes in Las Vegas, and the Lewis and Ross families in San Bernardino. These entrepreneurs were inspirational to me because of their success, and also their vision. A common denominator among them was that they'd seem to have started buying up land, not necessarily in existing metropolitan areas, but in areas where development had yet to happen.

By studying them, I knew that in order to become a successful landowner in Southern California, I had to answer one very important question:

Where is the next path of growth and development?

Knowing that I needed to buy based on affordability and availability, I began to research various areas to pinpoint the path of growth. Seeing as Southern California has approximately 60 percent of the state's population, and the population was migrating east, I began to research various areas along the 15 Freeway. I traveled frequently along the 15 Freeway from San Diego toward Mira Mesa, Temecula, Murrieta, Corona, Ontario, and Rancho Cucamonga. The

15 Freeway is not only widely considered to be the busiest economic corridor in the West, but is familiar to most people as the route to Las Vegas, both pluses for land speculation. I saw growth potential in San Bernardino County and wondered how much of the vacant land was actually up for grabs.

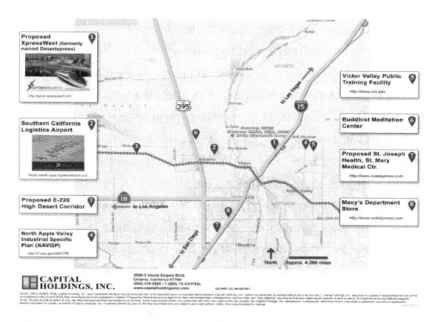

Nos. 1-8: Approximate location of some of the major existing and planned developments in the High Desert.

I learned that approximately 81 percent of the land in San Bernardino County, California was owned by the government, approximately four percent by cement companies, and maybe another four percent by the railroad industry. Take away the land that can't be developed (mountains, washes, etc.), existing and dedicated roads, already developed areas, lands owned by private owners and developers, and there was relatively little available for purchase.

Land, just like anything else, follows the basic law of economics: the lower the supply, the higher the demand, and the higher the price.

Given that undeveloped land is almost unheard of in the heart of San Diego and Los Angeles, the flow of Southern California development was heading eastward, specifically toward the Victor Valley, a beautiful, scenic desert area with clean air, and a location with enough affordable, flat land to make it the next major metropolitan area in the region.

In 1999, the town of Victorville, in the heart of Victor Valley, was economically depressed as a result of the closure of George Air Force Base. Thousands of jobs had been lost, and real estate values were at an all-time low. According to some of the locals, the area was also dealing with an upsurge of meth production. While such setbacks sent most investors looking elsewhere, I had a feeling I might have hit proverbial pay dirt. I researched the area further, learned the topography, read local newspaper articles, and attended city meetings to determine whether this region had any or all of the precursors of growth necessary to rebuild, develop, and realize the potential that I envisioned in this area.

What exactly are the Precursors of Growth?

1. Accessibility
2. Utilities
3. Airports and Transportation
4. Development and Expansion in the Region

In 1999, I analyzed the Victor Valley in light of each of the precursors of growth and determined the following:

1. Accessibility:

Although relatively remote by California standards, the High Desert, where the Victor Valley is located, is easily accessible to the Los Angeles basin and about a two-hour drive from the rest of Southern California via Interstate 15, which goes south to San Diego and north to Las Vegas. The Victor Valley segment of the I-15 experienced at least 60,000 cars on a daily basis. Other major freeways and arteries that linked Southern California with the cities of Victor Valley were, and are, Highway 395 to Canada, and Highways 18 and 138.

2. Utilities:

Utilities like water and power are all critical precursors for growth. The Victor Valley boasts easy access to the California Aqueduct and an efficient existing power structure, and plans were also underway for an 830-megawatt, natural gas-fired combined cycle power plant able to provide power for 800,000 residential customers.

3. Airports and Transportation:

Airports are major catalysts for growth. In Southern California, airports like LAX, San Diego, John Wayne, and Ontario (which started as a logistics airport to decongest air cargo traffic in and around L.A.) have facilitated unprecedented and continued growth in the cities surrounding them. While the impact and necessity of LAX speaks for itself, John Wayne Airport demonstrates a successful blueprint for growth and city planning. Ontario Airport, which was originally designed to handle 20 percent of the cargo flights from LAX, evolved into an international airport. As a result, there are now a lot of manufacturing and industrial companies in the area.

In 1999, Victorville was economically depressed after an estimated 10,000 jobs disappeared as the result of the closure of George Air Force Base. The silver lining, however, was that the base was in the process of being converted into the Southern California Logistics Airport, also known as Global Access. This 8,500-acre property, which is over twice the size of LAX, was created to be a multi-modal freight transportation hub supported by air, ground, and rail connections. It would be the largest fully integrated commercial development in the area, and designed to handle approximately 80 percent of cargo flights coming into LAX. I was convinced that SCLA in Victorville was positioned to be a major inland port of entry.

Ontario Airport created a tremendous number of manufacturing jobs. It then created a huge demand for housing in the area that was much less costly than homes in Los Angeles. When population in the Inland Empire grew as a result, it made sense for airline companies to offer charter flights, domestic flights, and eventually international flights.

This seems to be a typical scenario—an airport starts to handle cargo, then charter flights, and then domestic and international flights follow. Since growth was continuing in the Inland Empire, there was a need for a new, nearby cargo airport. The Southern California Logistics Airport, located just on the other side of Ontario's San Gabriel Mountains, appeared to be exactly that place.

Ontario International Airport Aerial :

Aerial Map from 1966: Historicalaerial.com - USGS (1966-04-16 - 1966-04-16)

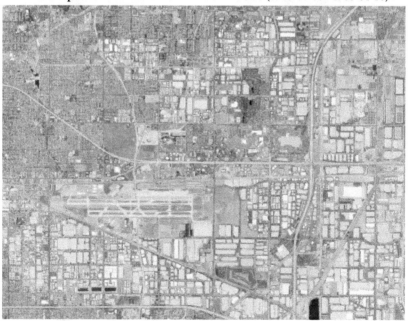

Aerial Map from 2012: Historicalaerial.com - USDA (2012-04-23 - 2012-07-20)

4. Development and Expansion in the Region:

Before 1999, for many people, including my family, Victorville was simply a fuel stop on the way to Las Vegas. According to the Census Bureau, population has steadily increased from 14,220 in 1980 to 40,674 in 1990, 60,000 in 1996 and 121,096 in 2013. It has grown steadily since, and is continuously growing, and a lot of people have made it their home. Victorville now has its own shopping mall, mini-malls on street corners, nationwide restaurant chains, and subdivisions sprouting everywhere. With cheap land, affordable housing, and a younger labor force now in the area, companies have started eyeing the High Desert for their expansion as well.

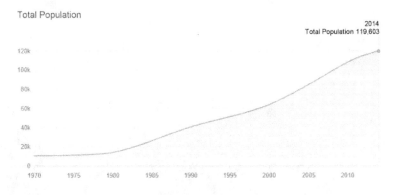

Victorville, CA Population Graph
http://places.mooseroots.com/l/316653/Victorville-CA

Victor Valley

The scenic, and beautiful Victor Valley clearly had all the precursors of growth to convince me it was the most affordable location with the best long-term investment potential for my investment dollars.

I started buying individual parcels in and around the towns of Victor Valley. I was buying vacant land with potential at a great price. I founded Capital Holdings and turned around some of the land for a profit, which enabled us to buy more. We bought parcels of various sizes, mostly one by one, and continue to enthusiastically do so today.

The Victor Valley, Then and Now

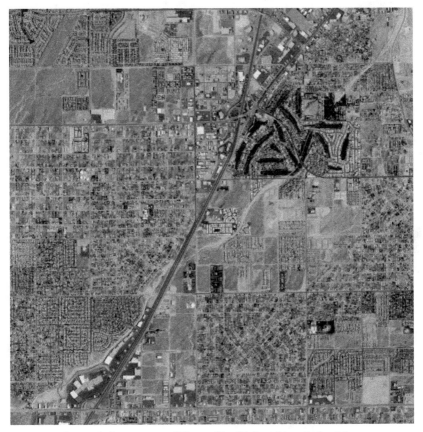

Before and after pictures of Victorville, CA from <u>historicalaerials.com</u>

As you can see, a lot has changed since 1999, and the area continues to grow.

People come out to the area expecting the Sahara Desert. While they will see plenty of sand, desert flora and fauna, many are surprised to see what else is happening—nationwide retailers, fast food chains, restaurants, and various industries. Not only have the seeds of development been planted, they are starting to sprout. Major commercial developments have already established themselves in the region including Walmart, General Electric, Dr. Pepper Snapple, Exel Logistics, Fastenal, Leading Edge, Newell Brands, Pacific Aviation

Group, Plastipak Packaging, Pratt & Whitney, Red Bull, Sparkletts, Solar City Corporation, United Furniture Industries, Boeing, Fed Ex, and a variety of others.

Nowadays, the success of companies depends quite heavily on their logistical efficiency. The key is being able to deliver products the fastest. I believe that the companies above have relocated in and around the SCLA because of the importance of logistics, and the increased ability to deliver products quickly by being situated adjacent to a cargo hub.

At 8,500 acres, SCLA is over twice the size of LAX. More jobs are anticipated in the region, which has brought an influx of families and the need for new homes and services to support the growing population.

In addition, plans based on existing, developed technology are underway for XpressWest, a high-speed train that will take passengers from Victorville to Las Vegas in 80 minutes, reaching speeds of 150 miles per hour. Aimed at reducing traffic-related stress and emissions on the I-15, XpressWest will one day connect to Los Angeles and the California High Speed Rail. It is anticipated to create over 80,000 direct and indirect construction-related jobs. In addition, initial work has started for the High Desert Corridor (HDC). City and state governments anticipate growth on both ends of Highway 14 and east of Freeway 15 (Palmdale and Apple Valley). Building the High Desert Corridor (Highway 220) will significantly help in the reduction of the numbers of cargo truck traffic on the I-210, I-10, CA-60, and CA-91. A new freeway and a high-speed train system will also create an alternative east-west corridor in the event of an emergency (i.e. an earthquake) in the Los Angeles basin.

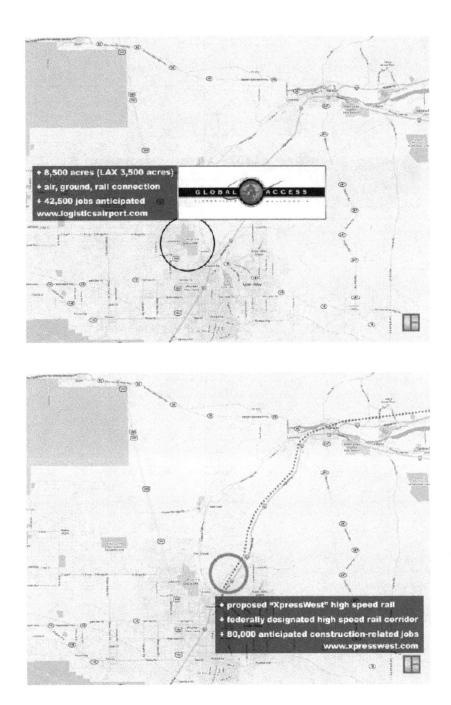

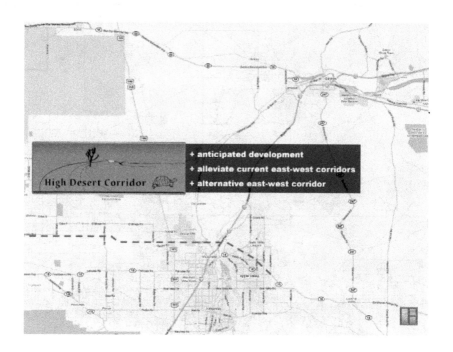

High Desert Corridor

+ anticipated development
+ alleviate current east-west corridors
+ alternative east-west corridor

CHAPTER FIVE

WHEN TO BUY LAND

Whenever I started a business venture, my family, especially my mom, would always remind me of the risks. My family wanted to make sure I didn't fail, and my mom just worried. My closest, well-meaning friends would also scrutinize whatever plans I had in mind. Although I didn't always see eye to eye with my loved ones when it comes to business, their concern was always appreciated. Over the years, they helped me calculate risks more thoroughly and helped me give deeper consideration to my decisions.

When they saw that I was ready to give up a stable, well-paying career to open Capital Holdings, many of my friends and relatives thought that buying land for myself was one thing, but starting a land business focused on an economically depressed "nowhere" seemed utterly insane. Needless to say, I felt otherwise. Having done the extensive research mentioned previously, I felt certain I was simply taking a necessary, short-term risk that would result in solid long-term gains.

In 1999, Capital Holdings opened with a limited but diverse inventory. I bought as much as I could, only purchasing smaller parcels of land that I felt would be affordable to many people. We worked diligently to turn them over as quickly as possible. We managed to sell many of the parcels to cash buyers and greatly exceeded our sales goal that first year.

Needless to say, my family and friends stopped questioning my sanity.

I was able to make an offer on a building in Oceanside across the street from our small office. Fortunately, our bid was not accepted. I say fortunately, because that denial led us into buying a building roughly half an hour away from the Victor Valley in the city of Rancho Cucamonga instead. As it turned out, living and working in Oceanside would have limited us to one or two tours of the Victor Valley for prospective clients per weekend. Opening an office closer to the Victor Valley enabled us to more than double our productivity.

In 2001, we bought a commercially zoned house on Main Street in Hesperia so we would have a place to meet clients in the High Desert. We bought a building in Rancho Cucamonga not too long after, knowing this was where we would be focusing for the long haul.

Over the last seventeen years, the High Desert has not only brought me success, but also a deep appreciation and love for the region. I totally believe in the area, which I think helps make other people I meet or who attend our presentations feel the same way. I will not sell something that I am not willing to buy myself. Currently, we own several commercial and residential properties and have finally built our first building in the area. While writing this book, I've started working with an architect to build my dream home in the Victor Valley.

When do I buy land?

As a land investment professional, a question I'm often asked is, "How do you know when it's the right time to buy land?"

The simple answer is: when you are in that place where you have done your research, you know where you want to buy, have the financial ability, and doing nothing is not going to be an option. That is the time to buy.

The trick is getting to that point in time at the *right* time.

In my opinion, there are a number of factors you need to consider before you invest in land. Assuming you have done all the research necessary and have narrowed down your target area based on the factors discussed in the previous chapter, including the presence of precursors of growth and an awareness of the path of development, you are ready to figure out exactly when the market is right for you.

Market Fluctuations

It seems like there is always talk of an impending recession, of the Chinese economy tanking, Europe being a mess, or the state of things in Brazil and Argentina. Often for good reason. The main thing to keep in mind is that recessions come and go, and downturns are normal, but the population never decreases. The market constantly changes, but the need for land doesn't. While real estate historically goes in ten- to fifteen-year cycles, people who were twenty-five years old when a recession starts will be in their thirties ten years later, and, despite the state of the economy, may have married, had a family, and are needing a home that will have to be built on a piece of land. Although the perception about the value of land may change depending on how the economy is doing, the need for it remains constant.

That said, there are some basic guidelines for the best time to buy and sell based on the prevailing economic climate:

Recession

In general, a recession is the best time to buy and the worst time to sell land because demand will be lower, which forces real estate values down. When the stock market is falling, that's not the time to sell either. Like the stock market, the ideal time to buy land is during a downturn or recession. More important, hold on to any real estate you already own and wait until the market rebounds. If you have a good return before that time, you can choose to cash out at some point along the way. You will likely lose money on your current investments if you sell too soon or too late.During the last recession, I noticed that Caltrans, the government agency that builds the roads and highways in California, was doing a lot of acquisition and acquiring land through eminent domain. Why? When the market is down, the State of California can acquire land using less tax dollars. I've jokingly asked a few officials if they come up with a recession every so often so they can buy on the cheap. Of course, I don't believe such a thing, but it's not all that far-fetched; the population keeps on growing and so does the need for more freeways and services, even during an economic downturn.

Booming Economy

Ideally, you should not buy land when the economy is booming because the cost of land will be at its peak. If you have property to sell, however, this is an ideal time to cash out. People have a tendency to think that real estate will continuously go up. While that is true in the long term, in the short run, fluctuation is the name of the game. At some point, the market will have to have a correction. It will go down. Incredible, fast expansion is not sustainable.

If you make the "mistake" of buying land just before the market corrects, remember, you made this decision based on many sound factors. Seeing as you are in it for the long haul, and land is a diminishing resource, hang on and you should be okay in time.

The most common mistake I see is that people buy or sell their land at the wrong time.

When the market is peaking (a lot more people are buying than selling), you must consider selling or sell, and not wait for the actual peak, which can be impossible to predict. The market is eventually going to have a correction. Some people tend to think that the market will just continue to go up and up, and that it can make them more and more profit. By the time they finally decide to sell, it is too late. Others assume that it won't take as long to recover as it actually does. Do not get caught in these scenarios, as real estate historically goes in ten- to fifteen-year cycles. Do you have the stomach for the ups and downs in real estate? If not, and you do not have a crystal ball, you may want to sell well before the market peaks and not wait for the possible maximum return or profit. It is better to get 50 percent or even less of something than 100 percent of nothing.

If there's a lesson that we must then learn, it is to wish for the best, but be ready for the worst.

Bumps in the Road

In 2008, we started construction of the Amargosa Building in Victorville. The building was approved for a construction loan, we'd signed the loan documents, and the schedule for funding was done.

Days before the ground-breaking, the bank called to let us know that they were no longer funding construction loans due to the impending recession. It was a shock, to say the least.

The people we were working with knew that we had a valid reason not to proceed, but we wanted to make good on our commitment to our contractor, architects, suppliers, and contract workers, so we decided to finance it ourselves.

In construction, a 10-15 percent overage on budget must be anticipated due to plan changes and unexpected delays. Since we honored our end of the deal by coming up with the money to go forward, everybody involved tried his very best to make sure that the building was built on time. Not only was it built ahead of schedule, but at 10 percent below budget!

In the end, it was the best example of what my dad had always reminded me: if I take care of others, I don't have to worry about myself. As soon as the building was finished, a large area was leased out to a health/medical provider—a blessing, considering the increasing vacancies due to the recession.

At Capital Holdings, we've thrived in the good times, and not only survived downturns but managed to stay solvent as many other real estate companies closed during the 2008 recession. I believe we were fortunate to have withstood the blow because we honored our obligations, and because we were not just depending on a few big accounts. We had structured the business so that we had numerous small and medium accounts that were not as badly affected by the recession. Payments were small enough to remain manageable for a lot of our clients during this time, and they didn't make much of a dent in their budgets. The big accounts were the ones that resulted in late payments and, eventually, cancellations. Many of them were owned by clients who were in businesses that were most affected by the recession, like upscale restaurant and spa owners. When people are in a saving mode, these types of businesses are first in line to feel the effects.

Since we were able to maintain our financial stability, and were confident about the viability of our location because of its accessibility, infrastructure, growth, and growing population, I once again focused on buying smaller amounts and selling to people who were able to take advantage of the market during this time. Seeing what our company was paying for land in a good market, it made sense to buy up as much as we could, and maintain a solid foundation with the expectation that the market would come back up again.

I also learned to hope for the best, but be as prepared as I could for the worst.

The market is good, but am I ready to buy?

The economic climate is right, you've located great land at a good price along the path of development, and better yet, it is in an area with the infrastructure to become a thriving metropolitan area. The time to buy appears to be now, but are you ready to be a speculative landowner?

Before you sign on the dotted line, you need to consider the following:

- **Do you have the discretionary income?**

What is comfortable for you to spend on both a down payment and a monthly outlay without pulling food off the table, or limiting your current or preferred lifestyle? While a potential financial gain is likely, land, like most investments, is speculative.

- **What can you afford to buy AND hang on to until you're ready to sell?**

Only buy what you can sustain, whether it is an up market or a down market. To make money, you only want to sell when the market is up, which means you need to be able to hang on to your property if and when the market dips.

- **Do you have the stomach for the inevitable fluctuations in the market?**

When buying land, you must have the stomach for volatility so you will not be surprised by, and in fact, expect, the downs as well as the ups. If it happened in the past, it can and will happen again. People who are able to hang on to their property do just fine. The moment you panic and sell in a down market, you lose. So, if you are going to get nervous, buying land may not be for you. You want to be able to afford to sustain your purchase and sell if you want or need to when the market comes back. While ideally, you should buy when most people are selling, and sell when most people are buying, it is just human nature for people to tend to do things when everybody else is doing them.

Do you have the confidence to trust the market, and not the actions of everyone else?

- **How is your business affected by fluctuations in the economy?**

If you are investing in land, you need to take a close look at the kind of business you are in. If you think that your industry will be affected tremendously in a downturn, and you won't have the means to sustain it until the next upturn, land investment can be a tricky proposition.

I had a client who was in the drapery business. She made beautiful window covers for new homes and model homes. She bought a thirty-acre piece of land from us for about $55k and she had a $280k offer from a builder at the peak. She didn't sell. The recession came, and her industry was totally affected because it was closely related to new home construction. Because her business was affected as much as it was, she could not keep up with the payments. We tried to help by offering accommodations we normally provide our clients, such as lengthening the terms to lower monthly payments, allowing temporary interest-only payments, or adding a partner of their choice. Despite all these accommodations, she unfortunately had to give up the property.

Another client bought a twenty-acre parcel in 2001 for $125K, and had a $2,000,000 offer in 2005, at the peak of the market. She is in the medical field, and her industry was not very much affected by the recession. People get sick no matter what the state of the economy. In fact, it may even be that more people get sick in a recession. She was still gainfully employed through the tough few years that followed. She refused to accept the $2,000,000 offer, and kept up her payments on the property. Builders are once again inquiring about her property. She will likely get a much higher offer this time. She may have made the right decision in not selling it.

Having seen the effects of the economy on various clients' businesses firsthand, I do ask people to take a closer look at the kind of business or industry they are in before they buy, and when deciding whether to sell or hang on to property they already own.

- **What is the right size?**

Once again, you need to decide what you can afford to put down and, more important, what you can afford to pay monthly for the long haul. Ideally, you want to make the most return on your investment, which may mean hanging on to the land for longer than you might have anticipated. Only buy as much as you can afford to pay without compromising your lifestyle.

Where are we now?

While I wish I had an actual crystal ball, land market tends to follow the housing market trend. Lately, we have more developers looking into land. Permits are being pulled and subdividing is happening more. The housing market is generally doing better. At its lowest, homes were selling in the Victor Valley for as low as $50-70 per square foot, which was lower than the cost of construction. Currently, I see homes selling at $100-150 per square foot. If it costs a builder $100 per square foot to build, being able to sell at $120-150 per square foot makes sense. I think we've hit the bottom, and believe our economy is getting a little better now.

As a result, I feel confident about recommending that people invest in land now, assuming the market price is comfortable for them, while anticipating the market fluctuations that can, and will, happen.

CHAPTER SIX

HOW TO BUY LAND

Before I started Capital Holdings, I did extensive research on the Victor Valley. I attended city meetings, drove on every city and dirt road, and talked to people who lived there. We stayed in the area for days and on weekends to thoroughly understand the neighborhoods in and around the cities. George Air Force Base had just closed and local residents were mostly negative about the area's possibilities. People working in the city and county offices I talked to were not much more encouraging.

I disagreed.

With a future commercial airport, a major economic corridor, the 15 Freeway, a plan to build a huge power plant, the presence of the California Aqueduct, and cheap land, I thought that it had all the makings of a possible boom town.

As a result, I opened Capital Holdings with a plan to:

1. Focus on the Victor Valley area.

2. Buy affordable, individual parcels of land.

I started buying land that was in a good location and way below market, one piece at a time. These parcels normally required an immediate close with almost no time allowed for due diligence. It was a "buyer beware" kind of situation, but we knew the area very well due to all the research we'd done. Because it was a cash-only business with little competition, we were able to acquire really prime, cheap parcels and pass on the savings to our clients.

I would then advertise parcels from as low as $10,000 for a very affordable $1,000 down payment and approximately $73 per month. I quickly found that city dwellers, many of whom lived in apartments because they couldn't afford property anywhere near where they lived, were hopeful and very excited about the opportunity to own a 2.5-acre parcel for such a price.

Sales were brisk and we were soon able to buy a commercially zoned home on Main Street in Hesperia, which we still own to this day. We would go there on a Friday afternoon or Saturday morning to meet people and do our presentations. Soon, clients were recommending us to people they knew. Agents who were working with us brought their own clients in to see our offerings.

I would make a presentation, and take prospective buyers out to the area for a tour. We would have breakfast, brunch, or lunch to experience the weather, and meet some people that lived there so they could get a general idea about life in the Victor Valley. We did one-on-one tours of this nature, as well as bigger tours with fifteen or more people. The advantage of the bigger groups is buyers were able to see a lot more properties. It also gave people comfort to know they weren't the only ones buying, which helped validate their land purchase. We found that we made a lot more sales that way, but there were disadvantages. For one thing, the tour took a lot longer. We even had an instance when a tour took so long, it grew dark, and we had to have flashlights! Big groups can also create bad blood when there is competition for a particular property, which happened quite a bit at the peak of the market.

I came to realize that the big group works best when you are selling in a subdivision where all the parcels are in one place—which wasn't our business model at all. In our case, each parcel was, and is, unique. I also realized that I really enjoyed short, focused, one-on-one and small group tours because they gave me time to really understand what each client wanted, needed, and could afford. As a result, I now insist on smaller groups, which gives us the opportunity to better qualify and understand our clients.

These days, I normally start my tours by asking questions about what potential clients are thinking, what is affordable, etc., so I can make the tour as efficient and effective as possible. I then map out our plan with any specific parcels they have in mind, and then show them other possibilities in their price range. It is always my goal for the client to enjoy the experience as much as I do, and, of course, make a land purchase that becomes a win-win for everyone.

The art of the speculative land deal

While I definitely bought (and continue to buy) by price, which led to purchases throughout the region, I tried to buy the bulk of the parcels closest to the major city to the south, which is Rancho Cucamonga, and have since worked my way north along the path of development. I try to own a parcel in almost every mile or within a three-mile radius in areas where I want to concentrate, so that I am notified by the city about anything that is worth knowing—like somebody applying for a permit, re-zoning, or road construction. I buy parcels, even if I know I may not be able to sell them anytime soon, if it will serve this purpose. Another reason I buy this way is that when a big developer is buying in an area, they have to buy us out to acquire the land they need. When I happen to own the small piece they need to complete their acquisition, it gives me very relevant information that I use to decide where to concentrate our future purchases.

At Capital Holdings, we do all the due diligence possible on the land we buy by checking the title, looking for anything unusual. That said, no matter how careful you are, something can be missed. Early on, we sold a piece of land with no physical indication of a buried gas pipeline. A client bought the parcel with plans to build a home. During the process, we learned that a pipeline was not only there, but in the middle of the parcel. Because of this, I refunded all monies, took the property back, and we worked out the issue with the title company ourselves. Our client decided to buy another piece in a different area. I learned from this experience that things can go wrong, no matter how much due diligence you do. As a result, I decided to keep two to three parcels in areas where I am selling to ensure that if something goes wrong with any land we've sold, we have the ability to replace it with a comparable or an even better parcel. This gives our clients additional confidence about their purchase, and our "insurance" properties have turned out to be some of our best investments.

One example is this ten-acre parcel:

I purchased this land in 2002 for $46,000. At that time there were no significant building plans in the area. As luck would have it, the land is now a corner property across from a huge hospital that is currently under construction. We were offered $2,500,000 for it in 2013, which we refused. Now, some are selling their land in the area for as high as $15 per square foot (for a ten-acre parcel, it would be around $6,500,000).

Because word continued to spread about us, we quickly outgrew the house on Main Street. That's when we bought our first two-story building along the 15 Freeway in Rancho Cucamonga. The building was partly industrial, and it wasn't a perfect fit for the sales operation we have. When I was offered a newly built building next to a hotel in Ontario and much closer to the Ontario International Airport often used by our clients, I thought it was time to move and finally have a place that could be specifically designed for our use. At the time we purchased our first building, there were very few buildings in the area. Now it is nearly filled up, with some vacant land that is mostly available only for lease. Eventually, we rented out the first building and the home in Hesperia (but not before buying the adjoining vacant lot, which we plan to build on or lease in the future) and moved to our now current 6,460 square-foot office in Ontario.

What we did was start really small in a 300 square-foot office; we bought the house on Main Street, and then bought the first building in Rancho Cucamonga. I made sure that we only purchased and moved as needed, and certainly only when we were able to afford to do so. I believe it is better to crawl, walk, and then run.

These days, having our main office in Ontario works very much to our advantage. Clients see what can happen in an area where you have an airport that also started as cargo airport. It helps them visualize what can happen to the Victor Valley. It is also an excellent meeting point for our clients coming from San Diego, Los Angeles, Orange County and the Palm Springs area. We also have a branch office in Victorville, which is a convenient place to meet clients coming from the Antelope Valley, Las Vegas, and the Northern California area.

In this business, you do have to take risks, but you make them as calculated as you possibly can. There are times when a seller has to sell and close fast, and they don't want to go through the listing process. I know the area well and can make a decision quickly because we most likely have walked or driven the area. We have looked at the major washes, and have all kinds of maps that can tell us the location, elevation, and more. I weigh the pros and cons and make a fast decision. If I make a call and offer cash, I stand by it, and will not back out on a deal. I've learned to rely on my instinct and reason. Not to say that I haven't made grand mistakes along the way, but they helped improve my process. The saying about "too much analysis leads to paralysis" is true. If someone wants to sell and wants a fast decision, they know that if they offer it to us and we agree to purchase, they can count on the deal to happen.

Some other land companies have started buying where we were buying. Our advantage, however, is the relationship we have established with people we've done business with through the years, and sellers who know we are trustworthy and that we pay all of our vendors in a timely manner.

We try our best. We deliver. It is the way we do business. Word of honor is a must. If you make a promise, do it. If you say it, mean it. I intend to be in this business for a long time, and plan to pass it on to our children. For me, doing my research, buying along the path of development, performing my due diligence, purchasing within my budget, and establishing myself and my reputation in the community where I've invested, have truly worked to my advantage. I believe this "magic" formula will reap a reward for anyone who is willing to put in the time and effort, and is willing to accept the inherent risk.

How to Buy Land: In brief

• For the maximum profit potential, start with raw, undeveloped land and identify the nearby catalysts for growth (be it airport, roads, businesses in the area, etc.) that will one day bring development and more people closer to your parcel.

• When you start seeing some infrastructure development (roads, utilities) nearby, that's when the profit window starts to narrow. It is still not too late, as you will enter the investment with significantly added value.

• A few, if not several years may pass, until finally an offer arrives to purchase your land for pre-development. Usually, this is where our clients see their investment come to fruition when they opt to sell the parcel. For a select few, a build-to-suit or lease agreement is made to develop the property. So, on top of the land value appreciating, the investment now provides a regular stream of income.

• Typically, construction development from draft planning to a completed structure can take anywhere from six months to one year. Afterwards, the land along with its improvement enters the secondary real estate market: this is where houses are being flipped, or retail and industrial space is leased.

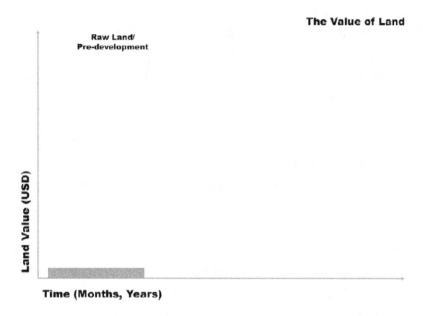

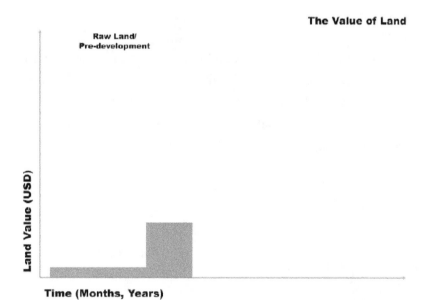

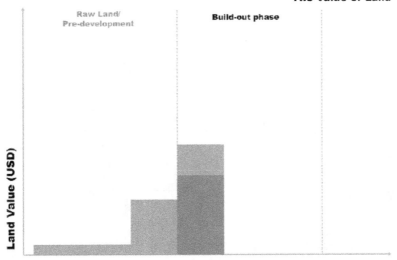

The Value of Land

Raw Land/
Pre-development

Build-out phase

Land Value (USD)

Time (Months, Years)

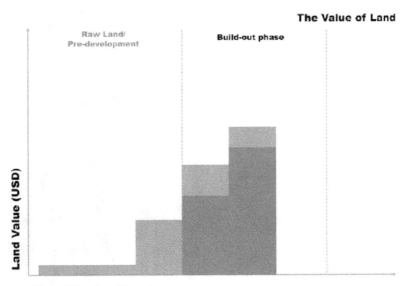

The Value of Land

Raw Land/
Pre-development

Build-out phase

Land Value (USD)

Time (Months, Years)

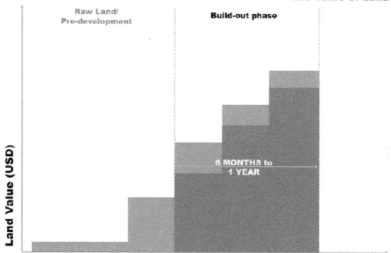

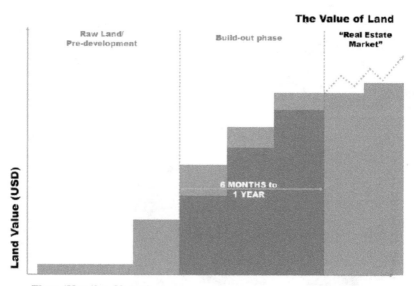

CHAPTER SEVEN

CAPITAL HOLDINGS, INCORPORATED

You now know why land is a good speculative investment. You know how I went about determining where and when to buy this valuable, limited resource. You not only know the steps I took (and take) before making a land purchase, but how I started and continue to maintain Capital Holdings so others can take advantage of the opportunity to own land. I hope I have created a successful model for speculative land investment. However, if you, like many people, don't have the capital to buy land outright with cash, but are still interested in what I truly believe is the best speculative investment in California, I'd like to tell you a little more about Capital Holdings and how we do business.

Capital Holdings, Inc. is a licensed, privately owned real estate corporation operating in California. Our specialty is selling raw, undeveloped land in a developing area. Since the company's creation in 1999, we have made land banking available and, more importantly, a successful financial venture for our clients. Our objective is to make land ownership available and affordable for everyone.

Facts about Capital Holdings
- Better Business Bureau member since 2001with an A+ rating
- Licensed with the California Bureau of Real Estate

- Strict and transparent business practices
- Remarkably knowledgeable about the area
- Expert guidance
- Large inventory of well-priced properties in a variety of price ranges, zonings, sizes, and locations—everything from small house lots to enough acreage to build a theme park
- Family-like atmosphere

As I've mentioned, we take clients through every step in the process to understand speculative land investing and its benefits by:

- Providing extensive reports and research of the area
- Obtaining city-specific potential development for each property
- Providing full disclosure and hazard reports
- Only providing parcels with clear and clean title
- Discussing the pros and cons specific to each client for each parcel

Along with our knowledge, guidance, and experience, we offer competitive loan packages with the following features:

- **Low 10 Percent Down Payment**

While most land companies offer some financing, most do not sell for as low as a 10 percent down payment. For example, we have 2.5-acre parcels available for $15,000, with a down payment of $1,500 and a monthly payment of about $137 (at 9 percent interest, payable in fifteen years). Terms like this allow more people to have the ability, courage, and willingness to speculate. For many, the decision is easier if they are investing with a dime rather than their whole dollar, especially during times of economic uncertainty.

- **No Qualifying**

When buying a home, one has to qualify for a loan because of the cost of improvement on the land. Land, however, is its own equity. With Capital Holdings Inc., there is no qualifying necessary for the buyer because the collateral is the land itself. Therefore, almost anyone can own land.

- **No Citizenship or Residency Requirements**

We advocate and encourage land ownership for anyone and everyone who is interested in our offerings. Fortunately, to buy land in California you don't need to be a citizen or a resident of the state.

- **In-House Financing**

Banks do not normally finance raw land. We do. We also operate by purchasing only what we can afford, so most of our transactions come out of our own pocket. In other words, we do not finance our clients through a financing company. We do it in-house.

- **Low Interest**

Depending on the down payment, we offer interest rates from five to nine percent APR. The higher the down payment, the lower the interest rate.

- **Terms For Up To Thirty Years**

We offer fully amortized loans. By carrying the note for up to thirty years, we can make the monthly payment low enough for a lot more people to own land. We have clients paying as little as $100-300 per month. Our payment structure also enables clients to hang on to their property until they are ready to sell. Though there is no guarantee that the same results will happen for everyone, some of our clients have received offers after two, five, or ten years and have sold their parcels for a good profit.

- **Bank Notes**

By maintaining all of our notes in-house, we can provide more flexibility. As with life, circumstances and budgets change and we try our best to assist clients experiencing financial hardship. If the notes were serviced by banks, clients with three to six months of non-payment could be cancelled or foreclosed. Fortunately, we can afford consideration and accommodations for our clients when necessary. Although we've been offered the opportunity to sell our notes, we've never sold one and do not intend to.

- **No Prepayment Penalty**

There is no penalty for paying off the note before the loan matures. In fact, we'd love the chance to celebrate with you when you sell it for a profit!

- **Exchanges**

At Capital Holdings, one of the things that truly set us apart from other land companies is the ability to exchange parcels. If a client changes his or her mind on the parcel purchased, we credit all of their down payment and principal payment to any other parcel of equal or greater value from our current inventory. Our exchange program makes the decision process a lot easier for some people. It gives them the chance to contemplate if they are choosing the right parcel for them. If they're going to lose sleep over purchasing land from us, then it's not a good deal for them, or us. Since we are financing the purchase for up to thirty years, we recognize it will be a long unhappy time for our clients to own a parcel that no longer fits their needs. Owning the land we sell enables us to offer this extra accommodation. We purchased the land first, so we don't mind getting it back via an exchange. Furthermore, we would not sell something that we aren't willing to keep.

- **Accommodations**

As I've mentioned, on a case-by-case basis, we can accommodate clients having financial difficulties longer than most financing companies by allowing temporary interest-only payment, adding a partner of their choice, refinancing for longer terms, or changing to a different parcel. Clients simply have to provide valid proof of the cause of the hardship they are having, and we are more than willing to help them keep their land. We do as much in the way of accommodations as we can before it reaches the foreclosure point. We want the best for our clients. We have total appreciation for the fact that the money they use to buy from Capital Holdings is hard-earned money too. Because we are in it together for the long haul, we want to do everything we can possibly do to see everybody win.

From the very beginning, I wanted to appeal to people of all income levels to invest in land. I try to have diverse accounts and not just big ones. Having small and medium manageable accounts has kept us in business and enabled us to keep our doors open, even during the last deep recession. Big accounts are great, but they can also have a big impact on the company if they cancel. It is unlikely that say, ten investors, whose investment is equal to one big one, will find themselves in bad financial situations all at once. After all, ten dimes also equal a dollar. For that reason, I've always preferred having many more clients owning smaller parcels of land as opposed to a few clients who own big parcels of land. A client who has bought a $49,000 piece of land for $4,900 down, with thirty-year terms and no prepayment penalty, gets an affordable investment that will hopefully yield a good return. I have found that those clients are the ones who stick in a downturn. Since we benefit from the income stream month after month, long-term notes are beneficial for both the company and our clients. It creates a win-win situation that has worked well for over seventeen years.

Additional Services

Over the years, we began to get involved with tenant improvement in the buildings we own. Later, we built a building in Victorville from the ground up. The building we are in today was a shell when we purchased it and had to be improved from the inside out. It is a fascinating process. We definitely have a better appreciation of construction after watching our contractors and architects do it. Going through the process of construction has made me better at assisting our clients who may want to build. My staff, and in particular my sons and daughter, have taken a special interest in developing projects. As a result, we've developed relationships with professionals who can assist or answer concerns and questions on entitlement, financing, design, architectural work, and construction.

Aerial View of the High Desert

Frequently Asked Questions

- **How much land must I buy?**

Our properties range in size from approximately 5,000 square feet to 320 acres. How much more you buy is up to you. We urge you to buy only what you can afford without spreading yourself too thin. While the whole idea is to make a profit, you have to assume you will be in it for the long haul. Land investment is speculative and there is no guarantee you will be able to sell or receive an offer a year, or even ten years, from purchase.

- **What about partnerships?**

Over the years, I've seen enough failed partnership arrangements to say I am not a fan. While it is ultimately a client's choice to buy from us with a partner, I actually discourage them. I would rather just put two (or three) people who want to buy land together into separate parcels they can afford on their own.

- **Your properties are located in the high desert. What is the area's normal temperature?**

The simple answer: a bit cooler than Las Vegas and a lot hotter than San Diego.

Summer: Low: 61 F (16C) High: 97 F (37C)

Winter: Low: 35 F (2C) High: 61 F (16C)

- **Are there facilities like hospitals, police stations, fire departments, schools, and grocery stores?**

Yes. Amenities, services, and schools are available now and continue to open. Due to the continuing increase in population, more schools, retail stores, etc. are currently being built.

- **Can I build on the property ASAP with just a 10 percent down payment?**

No. We require that the land be paid off in order to build. Most banks also require that land be paid off in order for them to approve a construction loan.

- **How much is the property tax?**

It is approximately one percent of value, plus bonded indebtedness. For the actual tax and more information, you will need to contact the respective County Assessor's Office where the parcel you are interested in is located.

- **What is the proof of purchase?**

It can either be an Agreement of Sale or a Grant Deed.

- **How can I be certain a property hasn't been sold to someone else?**

One can check at the County Assessor's Office as to who owns a parcel.

- **What area do you consider the best?**

The best area for you must depend on your budget, investment goals and timeline.

Accountability

I believe you have to be accountable for all that you do—both personally and professionally. At Capital Holdings, we are a family company with long-time employees we consider to be family. As such, I am totally accountable to everyone we do business with, and for my staff and agents. I have spent years engendering trust within the local community, and expect the same of everyone who works with us.

That trust has paid off in countless ways, from hearing about upcoming properties for sale ahead of the public to the generally accepted opinion that we not only keep our promises, but always take steps to correct any of the sometimes inevitable mistakes or miscommunications that can and sometimes do happen in the midst of a business transaction.

As for our clients, I've mentioned that I always keep two to three properties in areas where I've made sales just in case there is a parcel that encounters problems. I don't run away from problems, especially if the issue involves the people to whom I owe my success. In fact, I try to think ahead and prepare for the unexpected. I intend to be in this business for a long time, and I intend to pass Capital Holdings along to my children. To that end, I try to do everything I can, from due diligence during acquisitions to only selling properties I'm willing to own myself. Besides, it's just good business to take care of your customers and the people around you the way you want to be taken care of.

My father used to say, "If you take care of others, you will automatically be taken care of."

It's a philosophy I've not only adopted but embraced.

High Desert Before and After Pictures:

Roy Rogers Drive – Victorville, CA Aerial Map from 2005: Historicalaerial.com - US Department of Agriculture (2005-05-29 - 2005-09-29)

Roy Rogers Drive – Victorville, CA Aerial Map (Est. Yr 2010): http://ublog.naiglobal.com/naicapital/2015/12/30/krispy-kreme-is-coming-to-victorville-california/

Jess Ranch Marketplace – Victorville, CA Aerial Map 2005: Historicalaerial.com - US Department of Agriculture (2005-05-29 - 2005-09-29)

Jess Ranch Marketplace – Victorville, CA Aerial Map 2012: Historicalaerial.com - USDA (2012-04-23 - 2012-07-20)

CHAPTER EIGHT

HOW TO BUY FROM CAPITAL HOLDINGS

A s someone who has spent many years in sales, there's nothing I disagree with more than a high-pressure sales presentation. Needless to say, that is not how we do things at Capital Holdings. Because we are typically embarking on a long-term relationship with our clients, we believe in honesty and transparency in all of our business practices. While some clients do come in with outside financing, and/or cash, most are looking to finance their purchase through us. Regardless, we have a procedure we typically follow.

Choosing a Parcel of Land

1. When a prospective client comes into the office, we:

Ask the client to determine his/her discretionary income per month.

If, for instance, they say $500, we will then recommend they also look at properties starting at around $300 per month, so they stay well within their budget.

2. Determine the client's long-term and/or short-term plan for the land.

Do they plan to hold on to it simply for investment purposes? How long do they expect they will hold on to the land before they will be interested in selling? Do they have commercial or residential development plans? And so on.

3. We ask, and offer assistance if necessary, to help determine which city/area/location the client is most interested in.

4. We work with the client to narrow down the list of potential properties to a few of the most likely prospects.

5. We check parcel, aerial, topographical, and assessor maps, then use Google to show the location and surrounding area.

6. We compute required down payment and monthly payment for each of the potential parcels of interest.

7. We take the client on a tour of the area, showing them the land, as well as adjoining areas and developments, if any, which may impact/enhance their area of interest.

Once a parcel is chosen, we discuss, explain, and fill out the necessary paperwork.

The Paperwork Process

Assuming the client is looking for financing through us, Capital Holdings uses the California Association of Realtors' Vacant Land Purchase Agreement form, in which escrow will be opened. Title will transfer to the buyer at the close of escrow.

By our company policy, a purchase made using the California Association of Realtors' Vacant Land Purchase Agreement needs to go through escrow, as the deed of trust needs to have a trustee assigned to it, a title policy generally needs to be obtained, and a grant deed needs to be executed in order to transfer title to the buyer. Although not a requirement to transfer title, it is highly recommended that the grant deed be recorded for public notice.

Here are the steps that are followed:

1. Prepare all other necessary documents and disclosures to send to escrow.

2. Open escrow/assign an escrow number.

3. Escrow prepares paperwork confirming agreed sales price, interest rates, etc., orders preliminary title reports, hazard disclosure reports, other disclosures and sends them to both us, the seller, and the client for approval.

4. Escrow prepares the grant deed executed by CHI or the affiliated company that owns the land, and an Installment Note and Deed of Trust executed by our client for the remaining balance after the down payment (if the purchase is not a full cash sale and seller financing is obtained).

5. The escrow company requests the funds from the buyer prior to the close of escrow and deposits it into their trust account.

6. Escrow records the grant deed and deed of trust (deed of trust only applies if seller financing is obtained).

7. Escrow closes—proceeds from the sale are released to us, the seller.

8. In 4-6 weeks, the county mails the original grant deed to the buyer. If applicable, the original installment note and deed of trust is sent to the seller for record keeping until the note is paid off. If it is a cash transaction, or outside financing is obtained, this step is the last to complete the transaction.

9. If there is a note, CHI or its affiliated company that owns the land, executes and records a Reconveyance with the County, releasing the debt/lien on the property once the note is paid off.

10. Client receives the original Reconveyance directly from the County.

If a client comes in with cash or has secured outside financing, the transaction is now complete, until they hopefully come back for more land or for our assistance with development. For those who have chosen to finance with us, however, we have made "legal" what we hope will be a long, happy, financially successful future together!

I am particularly proud of the thank-you notes, comments, and testimonials we get from prospective buyers and longtime clients alike.

Here are just a few:

The meeting today was very informative, professional, and first class. We have high regard for Jet Sison and her business. ~ Flora D.

I recommend Ms. Sison and Capital Holdings Incorporated without reservation. In the business world, it is a rare opportunity to work with a true professional and an expert on a continuing basis. ~ William Y.

We are privileged to be doing business with your company. The properties you sell are all researched and studied so we have peace of mind knowing we can build on it. ~ Audie Y.

In an era where trust and exceptional one-to-one customer service excellence has virtually disappeared from our industry, the work Ms. Sison and her team did should be held up as an example for others to try to emulate. ~ Wendy A.

I thank Jet Sison and Capital Holdings for giving us the opportunity to become landowners in areas of potentially significant growth. ~ Salvador A.

I have really enjoyed working with Capital Holdings. Jet and all the staff were friendly and made my transactions easy. The property was better than I imagined and the earnings were just as explained. I made more in a year of holding the property than in the stock market or any other investments. Capital Holdings made obtaining and owning property affordable and accessible. ~ Diana C.

I have been working with Jet Sison of Capital Holdings for several years. I appreciate Jet's professionalism, knowledge, and efforts in working out land transactions in a most efficient way. I look forward to a continued and mutually successful working relationship with Jet. ~ Sharad M.

I would like to say with all sincerity that you have made my dreams into possibilities. ~ Vene T.

It is a great time to buy. Call Jet Sison, a Master in Land Investment. ~ Leo D.

Chapter Nine

Giving Back

At a very young age, I realized that life could be very different from one family to the next. Back in the Philippines, my parents were both employed, so we were considered middle class. As a result, we had both well-to-do friends and very poor ones. My mom taught in a school where most of the town's residents were farmers with next to nothing. My first few years were spent with kids who had very little. My parents, particularly my dad, encouraged me to share and be generous with others. I gave away my used toys, used slippers, and shared my lunch, paper, pencil, crayons—whatever I had that they did not—with my friends. I found it made them happy, but made me even happier. Sharing what I had made me look forward to seeing my school friends after a weekend at home. Seeing what I saw, I wondered why some people had so much, while others barely scraped by. My parents' explanation of the inequalities of life in the Philippines, and other places in the world, made me dream of doing whatever I could to help people in need.

The fire at our own home permanently seared that message into me. Losing everything gave me a unique and painful perspective about those who were even less fortunate than we suddenly became. Not only did I know what having nothing felt like, I learned about grace and generosity from the people who helped us out. By receiving when we were most in need, I realized how important it was to give a hand to others. The help we received also made me realize I couldn't live a happy, complete, content life without giving back.As a teenager, living away from my parents while I went to school, I kept myself busy by volunteering. I taught family planning in the slums of Manila, where some people had upwards of ten kids. I collected toothbrushes, soap, and other toiletries from private companies and distributed them in a correctional facility, where the inmates didn't even have the most basic personal grooming products. Volunteering and helping others made me feel less bitter about what I (and we as a family) had gone through. I always wondered why our home burned down, and certainly felt sorry for myself at times. However, seeing how so many people were forced to live made our misfortune pale in comparison.

I met a lot of kids in the slums in Manila who were very smart, but were not given the chance to go to school. They wanted to work, but no one would hire them. It was (and is) sad to see how many families lived on the street, sleeping on cardboard or in carts covered with only cloth or plastic to protect them from the elements. It's amazing how much most of us take everyday things for granted— simple things like soap, shampoo, hot water, having light by just flipping a switch, driving a decent car on a well-paved road, and mostly, not worrying where to get our next meal.

By helping others, I helped myself tremendously. It made me appreciate the littlest things. I learned that if you help nurse other people's pain, you forget yours. More important, doing for others gives you purpose, happiness, and appreciation for whatever you have, wherever you are. Ever since we settled in the United States, I've traveled back to the Philippines with suitcases full of clothing, books, magazines, food, toys—really anything I could part with to help provide some of the same comforts and blessings my family and I have enjoyed as citizens of this country. Sharing makes me appreciate the most mundane things we take for granted. For instance, giving away a lot of the clothes in my packed closet makes my closet more organized and saves me time in choosing what to wear, but also gives me a happy heart. I know the clothes I gave away are being worn well. I love knowing the used books that were collecting dust at our home are being read. Magazines we would simply throw away are treasured by those hungry for information about the world. Before I started using multifocal lenses, I used to have reading glasses all over the place. One time, I collected all my old reading glasses and handed them out to people my age. I was amazed by how appreciative people were of being able to see up close and read.

As the business grows, we are very fortunate to have been able to make more donations. Rather than celebrating a milestone birthday with a big, elaborate party, I prefer taking a trip home and using the money we would have spent on food for the hungry. Around Christmas time, rather than buying gifts just for our kids, we try to share with the homeless or fly back to the Philippines to spend the bulk of our holiday budget on those who need it most.

I make sure that my children are involved in charity giving. This is the reason why we plan to simply have leases on some of our parcels. This will enable them to have a regular source of income and always have the ability to donate and help others. This will also ensure that we can continue to help others long after we are gone.

Buoy Up Foundation

With the success of Capital Holdings, we were able to establish the Buoy Up Foundation to help others, and to help others help themselves. Located in Manila during its operation, Buoy Up Foundation provided food, clothing, diapers, gifts, toys, curtains, bedding, and whatever else we were able to provide. We bought a townhouse in the commercial section of Manila to serve as our office for the foundation. Initially, my hope was that street people could shower there because it has four useable bathrooms. I planned to stock it with soap, toothbrushes, and clean clothes. To be able to shower and use a bathroom is a very basic need, and a lot of people don't even have that. Unfortunately, the townhouse association would not allow us to use it for that purpose. I look forward to acquiring a place where there will be no such restriction.

Like many of the other obstacles I've faced, being told I can't do something makes me that much more determined to figure out how to succeed bigger and better. This is a daunting task when you see the enormous poverty in my home country. Providing food for people and giving them a place to shower is a temporary fix. It is very rewarding to give food and supplies, but as soon as the sack of rice and the canned goods are used up, what's next? I sometimes question whether what we are doing is making a dent at all. My ultimate goal is to be able to make a long, sustainable change in people's lives. We've tried a variety of different ways of helping, most of which involve delivering food and necessary items directly to the people in the slums. We've done it ourselves because we want to be able to reach out directly to people in need.

Over time, I realized that operating and managing the foundation ourselves required a lot more than what was feasible. For now, we provide assistance to trustworthy, already existing organizations that are doing great things that share our common mission.

I am also seeing the obvious: teaching people to fish as opposed to giving them fish is the best way to bring about permanent change. Helping more kids get an education may very well be what we must do next. For instance, if you have ten students who become nurses, teachers, or accountants, they will then be able to provide for their own families and also help others. I want to be able to make this happen for young people who are interested in education and public service. We plan to fund full scholarships that will not require the student recipients to pay us any money back, but to pay it forward by helping someone else once they are employed. My parents were adamant about our going to school. Education was our ticket out of poverty. I see how big a difference education played in my life as well as the lives of my siblings. We all want our kids to go to the best schools, live in a good home, and enjoy good food. We always want the best for our family. Since we have been able to provide that and more for our own children, I want to be able to give the best to as many people as I can. To do so, I have come up with what my friends and family might consider to be one of my most crazy, impossible ideas...

The Asia in America Project

The Asia in America Project, which I've been imagining ever since I started in the land business, is not only my ultimate goal; it is my plan and absolute purpose for my retirement and future.

Asia in America is based on an EPCOT type, multifaceted theme park concept where people will visit and learn about the culture of various Asian countries and the rest of the world. The goal of the Asia in America Project is to develop a world-class, multicultural, Asian immersion park experience in Southern California—a theme park with areas devoted to each major Asian country: China, Korea, Japan, Philippines, Vietnam, India, Thailand, Singapore, Malaysia, Indonesia, Pakistan, Laos, Cambodia. Each year, one or two areas will be allocated as "guest country locations" that would showcase other countries throughout the world including in the Middle East, Africa, and Europe.

Asia in America will showcase what all of these countries are about. There will be restaurants serving authentic food from each country. Products from each country will be available. The rotating guest countries will give visitors a new experience each year, and give them a chance to have better understanding of people all over the world.

Being in the land industry gave me the chance to meet people from different countries. I have clients from Dubai, Nigeria, Australia, Canada, Pakistan, India, Africa, and South America, and hearing their stories is awesome. Meeting people is fascinating, and I totally feel blessed to have been given the chance to know and understand a variety of cultures. As I have mentioned before, people may talk differently, dress differently, and eat different food from us, but we are all the same in our basic needs and desires for ourselves and our families. I know I had preconceived notions about people from other places that turned out to be completely wrong. I believe that having a place like Asia in America will give others the chance to do the same. Learning and eating authentic food from various places is something I think people must be given the chance to experience. Not everyone has the ability to travel to these places, so it will be great to have a place where one can have a "sampler" of various Asian countries, and countries all over the world.

Each separate country area will include the following components:
- **A museum hosting displays of the cultural, archeological, and historical heritage of the country**
- **An indoor/outdoor performance venue consisting of an amphitheater and an indoor theater appropriate for musical, dramatic, and motion picture presentations**
- **A commercial street where country-appropriate goods and services will be available for sale**
- **Restaurants serving authentic food from each country**

One of the main purpose of this project is to foster better understanding of the rich, diverse Asian cultures and the world, through education and direct experience of multiple art forms.

Added to my motivation is the potential business aspect of a project of this scope. I believe Asia in America will help make the High Desert/Victor Valley a destination. I also believe Asia in America will be a win-win that will help create jobs and revenue for the region.

Although it will be a while before my dream is a reality, we have made progress. We have set aside approximately 172 acres along Hwy 395 near the SCLA airport in Victorville, California. We have the conceptual drawings and a general business plan prepared. We have had our initial meeting with the various county departments that will have to work with us on the project. I met with the Philippine consulate office, and were willing to help put together the Philippines side of this project.

I anticipate that it may take years to get the project up and running. To help fund it, I have set aside parcels near the airport and other profitable locations where I plan to lease to fast-food chains, restaurants, hotels, etc. Once Asia in America is up and running, my hope is to lease the land to the various countries involved, with the income going directly to an education scholarship fund and other charities.

The idea of having a chance to educate and help others motivates me the most. I have been given an enormous opportunity and must pay it forward.

On those inevitable days when a snag occurs that seems insurmountable, or the task seems downright impossible, I think about a little boy I met in a Philippine orphanage. I asked him what he wanted. He told me he wanted lots of ice cream. I came back the following day with buckets of ice cream, and I saw how he made sure that everybody had their ice cream first before he started eating his.

I asked if he wanted to come with us when we went back to America, though I didn't think he knew what and where America was.

He said, "Only if I can bring my friends with me."

It was just amazing to me that this kid already understood the joy of sharing and thinking about others.

His spirit gives me spirit.

CHAPTER TEN

THOUGHTS ABOUT LAND AND LIFE

Cake is fun to eat with others. Eating it by yourself will not only make you fat, it can also give you diabetes...

When water is choppy, anchor yourself...

Everyone is on a journey to find their pot of gold, so the most travelled path will have the least return. Never be afraid to make your own path that others may use as well...

Never bet more than what will make you lose sleep...

Be in the game as much as you can, for as long as you can. The people watching may call you names or judge you, but in the end, they aren't the ones with the chance to win...

Be careful whom you ask for their opinion. Oftentimes, they are giving you what you want to hear, not what you need to hear...

My family and friends call these and the many other bits of wisdom I've been known to share at home and at the office, "Jettisms." They have given me a framework to live and work by that I believe has resulted in a fuller, happier, more meaningful life and career. I also believe that personal happiness and business success are interconnected.

I am often asked about how and why I built Capital Holdings, as well as my "tricks of the trade." Seeing as I've spent the bulk of this book outlining how I conduct land deals, I felt it only fitting that I wrap things up with some thoughts about the philosophies and experiences I've learned that have led me to where I am today.

"Jettisms" for Business and Life

1. Believe that you can, and you will.

Everything starts with you. You will never travel the distance without first believing you can. Having faith in what you can do is a must before you can convince others. Your mindset and clarity of purpose are very important in order to succeed.

The first time I saw a Porsche in a *Reader's Digest*, I imagined driving it myself. As time progressed, so did my dreams. I pictured having a beautiful home for my parents, working in my own office, managing my own business, and being able to help others. These scenarios played over and over in my mind. Considering I was just a little kid living in a house with no roof when I concocted these dreams, it may as well have been a wish for the impossible. At first, I kept a lot of these thoughts to myself, but eventually I shared them with my father and grandfather, who encouraged me to tell them my dreams. It was great to have two people whom I adored so much believe in me. I believe that sharing my hopes and dreams aloud set my mind and body in motion and enabled my dreams to become reality.

2. Each day will be as bright, as good, and as beneficial as you want it to be.

You have the choice, so why not make the decision to be happy? I realize that how my day will unfold is entirely up to me. If you think of your day as beautiful, it is. If you try to greet each day, no matter what the weather, with a big smile, your outlook will inevitably be brighter.

When something bad happens—say someone leaves you—it is your choice to be sad, sulk, wallow in self-pity, and feel unworthy. You also have the choice to congratulate yourself for ending a bad relationship, putting an end to wasting your time and emotions, and opening yourself to the opportunity of finally finding the right person. Whether you make such an event a "poor me" situation or a "hallelujah, I deserve better" is all up to you!

By the same token, I recognize that my mood can affect the people around me. Nobody wants to be around a glum person. If I am having a hard time and can't overcome my rainy day blues, I normally choose to be alone, write, or watch a movie by myself. I have no right to ruin somebody else's day.

It is easy to get frustrated when things don't necessarily go the way I want them to. Reminding myself that I have no control over a lot of things, and that I can only control how I react to them, helps me keep things in perspective. I take charge of how I feel. I do not let the weather or opinions of others define how my day is going to be.

In order to have the best day possible, I exercise, make calls, submit offers, and get the hard stuff done early in the day and enjoy what unfolds from there. It is much easier to deal with whatever needs to be done than to procrastinate. If it is too big a goal or project, I try to divide it into smaller, manageable pieces. I find that taking on the biggest decision first thing in the day not only works, but it also makes the rest of the day easier and more fun.

Mostly, I try to have fun in whatever I do. I try to make sure that I have as many belly laughs as I can every day. Opportunities are everywhere. Love what you do, even with its imperfections, or find something else that you will. Be where you are, and it will all be there.

3. Say it. Mean it!

Nothing makes you lose credibility and respect more than saying things you do not mean. Don't make empty promises, especially to yourself. If you say you will work out, do it! Maybe no one else will know, but YOU WILL! If you cannot trust yourself, who can? If you know you can't or won't do something, don't say you will. It's always better to under promise and over deliver.

4. Life nuggets are all around us.

We tend to focus on and seek out the most successful people, so much so that we miss the ability to learn from all the people that come into our lives. Everyone has something to offer—be it somebody you want to be, or somebody you would not want to become. I learn and expand my knowledge through everyone I meet and everything I do.

5. Be respectful of other people's truth.

We all come from diverse beginnings. We are products of different environments, and are shaped by different life experiences. What motivates you may not be the motivation for others. To expect others to totally appreciate your perspective on every topic is asking for trouble. If you are talking to someone face to face, remember you are looking at each other from different vistas, and there are various angles from which you can enjoy a particular view. Try to understand where others are coming from and avoid listening only to what you want to hear.

Being open-minded helps me understand my clients. I once made a presentation to a group of very well dressed city officials. One gentleman, seated at the back, seemed different. He was casually dressed in a t-shirt and slippers. After the presentation, the normal questions were raised. When everyone was almost ready to leave, he approached me with questions about a certain property and what I thought would be best for his budget—meaning he was interested. The following morning, I was awakened by the hotel staff and found him waiting at the lobby with a cash payment for what I recommended. Had I been judgmental, I'd have assumed he was the least likely as opposed to the most likely to buy, and would have lost him as a client. I have also learned that not everyone is going to be a client. Trying to convince everyone to agree with my point of view is not only pointless; it's unnecessary. Some people are more interested in stocks than investing in land, and that's a good thing. We need investors in the stock market to drive our economy. I accept that I cannot convince everybody. I just do my best, give it my all, and leave it at that. I do, however, give everybody the benefit of the doubt and always treat everyone the way I want to be treated.

6. Share what you know. Give what you can.

Sharing knowledge and information to help others can be very rewarding. Strive to inform; it will make the world that you are living in better! Never scrimp on what you know. Always give it your all! If you give and you share, you will automatically give yourself the chance to replenish and not stagnate.

I believe that selflessness is the most gratifying experience you can give yourself. Never be stingy with what you know, or what you have— it will create a bigger space for you to receive more in abundance. Take care of others and you will be taken care of without even trying.

Nothing makes me feel happier than being of help and benefit to others.

7. It's all about relationships.

In any business, you need to network to find people that could become your clients. Creating true friendships and valuing these relationships is the best thing I have done for our business and myself. The clients who became my friends have become my best referral source. This is good for our company, and it is very rewarding personally. This makes me enjoy my business tremendously. My clients are not just my clients. I consider them extended family and true friends. I never lose sight of the fact that they can buy land with an-other company, but they choose to do business with us. For that, I am always grateful. I love people, and lucky for me, this country offers an opportunity to learn from people from very diverse backgrounds. I enjoy forging real relationships and friendships with people from various cultures. It makes my job so much more interesting and fun!

8. Love yourself.

I grew up with a mom who told me to love myself. I didn't really fully understand what that meant at the time, but as I've gone through life, the message has become clearer. You cannot give what you do not have. You cannot water a plant with an empty bucket. Too many times, we are nicer to others than we are to ourselves. We dress up nicely for other people, and use better towels and dishes when we have visitors. Why not use the best for yourself? It will elevate your standards to the point where you will not have to make an effort to-ward others because it is simply how you are! When you know who you are, and love your authentic, original self, you will always be the best version of you.

9. Own up to your mistakes.

Mistakes are an essential element of growing up and a path towards perfecting your processes. Failures are the most valuable learning opportunities. When you make a mistake, own it! People who blame others for their mistakes may think that they are making themselves look better. On the contrary, it makes them look weak and cowardly.

"Sorry" is a very powerful word, and it has the vast ability to save you a lot of heartache. Nobody is perfect. No one! Pride will cost you pain. If, like me, you have been guilty of having to be right and prove others wrong, let go! Remember, there is no single way to look at or do things. Everyone has the right to their opinion—respect theirs, and they will likely respect yours. Apologizing will not diminish you in anyone's eyes. Instead, it will earn respect.

10. Gratitude brings opportunity.

Be appreciative, thankful, and grateful. Nobody owes you anything. When you learn to be grateful, blessings can be boundless. Being thankful for what you have, instead of agonizing over what you think you ought to have, will allow you to enjoy your enormous life. Too many times, we look forward to what might happen and fail to enjoy what *is* happening.

I feel very blessed to have experienced my humble beginnings. Where I've been has given me appreciation for a lot of the things I now have in my life. I believe it also gave me the drive to better myself and help others.

11. Treat everyone equally, and with respect.

Never ever think that you deserve better than others. If you want the best for yourself, your children, and your community, shouldn't others feel the same way? Realize that we all want to send our children to the best schools, give our family and friends the best that we can provide, live in a nice home, drive a nice car, and travel to our favorite places. If anything, we must look after those who are not as fortunate, or as strong. Everyone deserves to be treated like you want to be treated. When people come to my presentation, I make sure that I am prepared. I have all the materials and appropriate parcels to offer that will meet the budget and needs of the clients coming in. I make sure that all my equipment is in working condition. I do research and read a lot on things that are relevant in my business, and impart as much as I know to our attendees. The fact is, they are giving me valuable time that they could be spending with their families, but they have chosen to spend it with me instead. I try my best to educate, give them a fun time, and make all of them walk away from our presentation having learned something. It makes me happy to enlighten people about an investment that could benefit their lives, whether they buy land through us or not.

I look at all the preparation I do as creating a library full of materials that I believe people should know or might be interested in knowing. When they leave, I want them to be empowered. I have to make sure that I have given my attendees something that will be valuable to them, now or in the future.

Even if I know they may not be ready to make a decision that day, or only one person has shown up, I will still do my best. I treat everyone the same. It doesn't matter if they are buying a million-dollar property or a $15,000 parcel of land. By consistently doing this, I have clients that call me back years after attending our presentation.

12. Attitude is contagious.

Notice that when you yawn, people around you start to yawn?

Your attitude impacts the people around you. Nothing is more contagious than attitude. If you exude joy, people will emulate your mood. Have a bad attitude, and it spreads even faster!

People gravitate to those who are happy, fun to be around, and smile, so laugh at yourself and do not take yourself too seriously. Make meeting you not a waste of time. I believe you should make giving hope to others your responsibility. Be the reason that somebody smiles each day. Acknowledge people. Find anything you can use for an honest compliment. Hug whenever you can—it is absolutely good for you. Make being useful to others, your community, and your world, your ultimate life goal.

13. Be decisive.

In life, decisions must be made. I find that the right decision is easy. If a decision requires you to lose sleep, give it thorough consideration—it may not be the right one.

If you make a decision and it ends up not being the right one, own it! Use making decisions, whether right or wrong, as an opportunity to learn. Always be decisive, though. Not making a decision is the worst decision.

In my line of work, decisions, big and small, are made every day. I do not necessarily make the correct choices all the time, but I've learned that the key is to make more right than wrong decisions. Looking back, I think the wrong decisions I've made were actually the stepping-stones I needed to increase my odds of making the right ones. Nothing is worse, however, than not making a decision or allowing someone else to be the reason why you will or will not do something.

14. Truth is easy.

Truth is simple, and uncomplicated. Stick with what is true to you. Do not fight it. If you have to convince yourself of something, you may not be living your true self.Once, we had to deal with a lawsuit. It was not something that kept me awake at night. I knew that detractors come in two forms—either they have a valid issue or they want attention. If what they say is true, they have the right to say so. If, however, they are not asserting the truth, there is no reason to worry about it.

I know what I did and did not do. I will not do anything illegal, or anything that will harm anybody, especially the very people who put food on my table. Just do things the right way, and there is nothing to worry about. I was warned that there's no guarantee of the outcome in court, but I've always believed that truth is easy. Other than the outrageous expense, it was all worth it to be completely exonerated.

It is during these trying times that you learn the most valuable lessons. Education may be costly, but ignorance will cost you more. Truth is easy to remember and lies beget more lies.

15. You attract possibilities if you emit them.

If you expect others to come to you, be open. If you want people to look at you, smile at you, and greet you, do it first. Positivity is a major attraction. You attract possibilities if you emit them. Provide possibilities for people, and your life will be full. Be happy for others—be truly happy for the success of others. Try to make a difference to all you meet, be it with a smile, a handshake, or a positive thought. Share, give, offer, provide.

Instead of feeling disadvantaged as a foreign-born woman in a male-dominated industry, I focused on the possibility people would remember me better; immigrants would relate to me just as I did to them. I thought of these possibilities as positives and was able to use them to my advantage.

In all things, I try to give endless possibilities, not limit abilities.

16. Impose and you lose.

When I am speaking, I am imparting what I already know. It is when I'm listening that I am learning a lot of what I do not know. Allowing people to voice their thoughts and opinions is what attracts people to you. If there's something that people have in common, it is the need to be right. Do not immediately shut down somebody's idea. Listen, agree that it is a good issue, compliment them for bringing it up, and share where you are coming from. Putting people in a corner makes them defensive, and gives them a reason to build a higher wall—a wall specifically designed to keep you on the other side.

I try to listen to what my clients are saying. It gives me direction on where to go, what to say, and gives me a better understanding of what they need. I will not have the opportunity to give them all that I know at one time, but that's where analyzing, understanding, and listening to attendees' needs becomes of importance. I truly believe the best way to effectively close any deal is to stop talking and start listening.

Just as important: never ask people to do, buy, or own something you are not willing to do, buy, or own yourself.

17. Adjust and conform to situations.

I believe it is best to be like water that follows the contour of wherever it is contained, or to be like bamboo that simply sways back and forth when a strong wind blows. The ability to go with the flow is a necessity in this world. Being rigid will make you break easily. Be flexible and embrace change; change will always be the one constant, so try, experiment, and be open to whatever comes your way.

Though I always expect the best, I am also ready for the worst. When I make a sale, I am ready should it cancel. I will always do my best to save a deal but I also know that it is a numbers game. Early on in my career in sales, I made nine sales in one day. I went home spending the money I would have earned in my head, what bills to pay, things to buy, etc. Before the three-day cancellation period was over, I was notified that all nine of my deals were canceling, not to mention two more (the ones who'd referred me to the nine now cancelled deals). I definitely lost sleep as a result of that day, but having gone through the experience, I learned to never count up chicks before they hatch.

Life is full of challenges. If you expect them, chances are you will get through them just fine.

18. Welcome Change.

Change can, and often does, make things better. It's okay not to follow trends and norms. Dare to be different. It is best to be a pioneer.

In business, it is most likely that you are not the first in your industry. A lot of other companies may be doing the same thing. You almost have to differentiate yourself from the rest. In my industry, I strive to be the company that offers the lowest down payment (10 percent) and finances the longest (up to thirty years) with no prepayment penalty. We require no qualifying, and that we make exchange of parcels possible. I realize that we are not offering clients a $100 item that makes the decision process easy. We offer a high-priced item that will need a long commitment from our buyers. Because of the leap of faith taken by my clients, I think it's crucial to break from norms and trends.

19. Practice Makes Perfect.

I do a lot of presentations, and having done them so many times makes me better at my craft. I have been asked a lot of questions and encountered objections in so many different ways that I feel ready for whatever is thrown at me. I still get nervous prior to each presentation, which I believe is a good thing and I do not mind. It keeps me from becoming complacent. Before I do a presentation, I try to do a little mind exercise. I will go in a room, bathroom, my car, or anywhere I can be alone to clear my head. I owe it to people attending my presentation to do my best. I continue to learn, and become more prepared each time. Time and practice give you confidence that people see when you speak. Interestingly, I've discovered that the more experienced you are, and the more you know, the fewer questions are asked.

20. Persistence, motivation, and compromise.

I worked in or owned several businesses before finally finding the right business for me. I've sold pastries, cosmetics, opened a clothing boutique, and more. It is because I've worked in, or run, so many different businesses that I have full appreciation and understanding of what I do now. I was bankrupt at one point, which was the lowest point I've ever felt. I cried and wallowed in self-pity for a few days, but my three children gave me the strength to get up and never give up until I found the right industry and business for myself.Loving what I do keeps me motivated. Knowing my reason and my endgame makes me want to go to work to do what is necessary to keep our business going. A lot comes from my appreciation of the opportunity that I am given. It keeps me motivated, knowing there are more talented and hard-working people out there who have to work harder to provide for their families. I know that I have been given a chance and I have no intention of wasting the opportunities I've been given.

Success in my business takes making calls, endless touring, building meaningful relationships, making sales presentations, reading, studying, strategizing, delegating, and following up. I know that I must have the discipline and self-control to do what is necessary to get things done. I enjoy staying up late to read and watch movies, but I do go to sleep early when I have a tour or commitment the following day. One habit that has helped me a lot is always having my work related materials ready before I go home. It has happened too many times that I get an unexpected meeting with an investor, builder, or referral. Being ready has helped me avoid unnecessarily stressful situations.

Success also means compromise. When we started, our business took up almost all of our weekends and our free time with our children. Having my parents to help us out made it easier. Still, it was time that I can never regain. In this regard, I now make it a point to spend as much time with our grown children as we can.

21. Building a team.

In all my businesses, I prefer making people want to work with me, not for me. It is impossible to do everything myself. Even if it were possible, I am not the best person for every task. I do recognize that there will always be someone who is better than me at any given activity, and I must know what and when to delegate. I also cross-train employees, because life happens: people get sick, emergencies occur, and it is not acceptable for clients to have to wait to have their concerns addressed until the one person who knows the answer to a particular question comes back.It is amazing how working with people you trust and respect makes running a business so worthwhile. I spend most of my waking hours with my staff, so it is crucial to know that we trust each other and have each other's backs. I am forever indebted to my husband, parents, children, and the people on my team. They will always be a part of who I am.

22. Have a full understanding of your business.

Having started our business in a 300 square-foot room, where I was the janitor, broker, marketer, receptionist, bookkeeper, I learned every aspect of my business. It is easy to justify all that is good because it is mine, and be naturally protective, but I also understand the need to be my own best critic. I try to make honest dissections and analysis of my business. I try to understand the ins and outs, the pros and cons, the great and not so great aspects of what we do. I have to have a total understanding of the needs of my clients. I have to sell the way I want to be sold. I have to be able to convince me if I were the buyer. It is good to see and hear various points of view to make sure I am seeing everything objectively, so I ask my children, husband, parents, and trusted friends and clients about how I can do things better. I ask for honest criticism and comments. Also, knowing my competitors and anticipating changes in the market are of tremendous help to the company and to my clients.

23. Share your victories.

I am totally aware that wherever I may be in life, I owe my success to my family, the people I work with, and people that I have met along the way. I am a summation of all the people that I have known. All the successes I've had were made possible by the people that shaped my beliefs, and the knowledge and support all these people have afforded me. There are no successful people without the help of others. None!

24. Life is like a slingshot.

Just like a slingshot (which happened to be one of my favorite toys growing up), the more you pull back, the further it goes. In life, the more setbacks you go through, the better prepared you are to handle challenges. To do so, you may need to change your attitudes toward:

Rejection—make it your friend.

Doubt—no more!

Money—can be used to do great things.

Self-worth—never compromise.

Faith—keeps you grounded.

Inquisitiveness—you'll only get your answer if you ask.

Family and Friends—make it all worthwhile.

Love—have lots of it!

25. Life is also like a baseball game.

Notice that people in the bleachers watching the game are the ones who ridicule and boo the players? Just remember that they are also the ones who are paying to watch the players play. Don't mind what detractors are saying; be in the game, and you will eventually hit a home run. Keep swinging and keep taking (calculated) chances!

Final Thoughts

I hope this book has resonated with you and that it has opened your eyes to see how easy and fulfilling land ownership can be. Today is the day to discover your purpose and forge an interesting journey. Along the way, don't forget to laugh, enjoy, and maintain a sense of wonder in this awesome world full of opportunity.

Tomorrow will simply be the day when you will wish that you'd done it yesterday!

CPSIA information can be obtained
at www.ICGtesting.com
Printed in the USA
LVHW080214170920
666318LV00010B/78/J